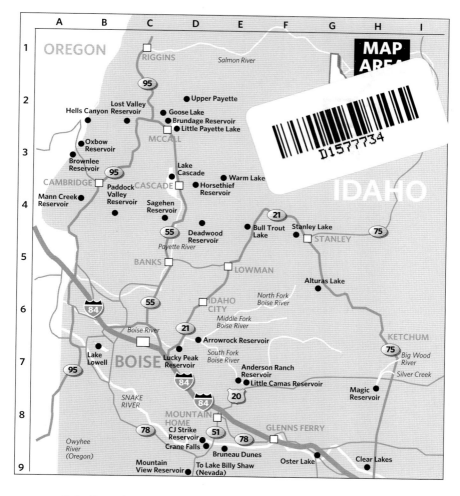

IDAHO STATESMAN PUBLICATIONS

# Southwest Idaho
# FISHING
# GUIDE

## 50 LAKES, RESERVOIRS, RIVERS AND PONDS
### PLUS EXPERT TIPS AND ANGLING TACTICS

## BY ROGER PHILLIPS & PETE ZIMOWSKY

President and Publisher: Mi-Ai Parrish
Editor and Vice President: Vicki Gowler
Editors: Jason Lantz, Bill Manny
Photos: Roger Phillips, Pete Zimowsky, Shawn Raecke,
Katherine Jones, Darin Oswald, Chris Butler, Kim O'Connor
Design and graphics: Patrick Davis, Tim Jones

**Idaho Statesman © 2010**

# Go Fishing!

Few places in the country have the excellent and diverse fishing options that Southwest Idaho offers. You can catch more than 20 different species of fish ranging from alligator-sized sturgeon in the murky depths of the Snake River to bluegill in a suburban pond.

You can catch cutthroats in cool mountain lakes that have stolen their color from the sky, cast flies to rainbows in world-famous Silver Creek, hook hard-fighting, sea-run steelhead in the mighty Salmon River, land a trophy smallmouth bass in Brownlee Reservoir or catch a bucket of crappie in C.J. Strike Reservoir.

Complementing those diverse fisheries is a climate that allows you to wet a line year-round.

Idaho Statesman outdoors reporters Roger Phillips and Pete Zimowsky have crisscrossed the region and fished most of these places or talked to experts who know them intimately and were willing to share their secrets.

This book will introduce you to the fish you can find throughout Southwest Idaho, the best time of year to catch them and what kind of bait or lures you should use.

It also includes a wealth of information about fishing tactics taken from experts with decades of experience fishing Idaho's waters, which will help make you a better angler no matter where you fish.

We had all anglers in mind, whether your idea of a perfect fishing day is casting flies in a gin-clear stream, trolling in a reservoir or sitting in a lawn chair next to a pond. And we didn't forget the beginners who are just getting started in this great sport.

With so much information available, you can learn more about your favorite fishing holes, seek out new ones, or try fishing for different species. You can also get the most current fishing information in the Idaho Outdoors fishing report every Thursday in the Idaho Statesman, or at www.idahostatesman.com/outdoors.

It's all right here, so we hope you take advantage of it.

Tight lines.

# Trout & cold-water fish

Rainbow trout

Trout are Idaho's favorite game fish, and there are five different species you can find in Southwest Idaho. They are the most widely distributed fish in the state, and inhabit nearly all waters. Add chinook salmon, kokanee salmon, steelhead (sea-run rainbow trout), as well as whitefish and sturgeon, and there's a lot of variety from which to plan your fishing trips.

## RAINBOW TROUT
These are the most prolific trout species in North America. They range from pan-sized to gargantuan and are found in all corners of Idaho.

The largest rainbow trout caught in Idaho was a 19-pounder from Hayden Lake in North Idaho. Trout in Southwest Idaho don't reach those epic sizes, but the area still has excellent trout waters.

Rainbows are considered the hardest-fighting trout and they are capable of impressive acrobatics when hooked. It's not uncommon to see a small trout clear the water several times in the course of a fight.

Rainbows are naturally aggressive and will eat almost anything — a worm, salmon eggs, cheese, corn, PowerBait, maggots, mealworms, insect larvae, minnows and crawdads.

Rainbows also eat all kinds of bugs, but that doesn't mean they are pushovers for anglers. In heavily fished waters, they can be extremely selective. There are few things more challenging, or frustrating, than a large rainbow feeding on the surface that absolutely ignores your false offerings.

### Rainbow tactics

Because of their diet and habitat, rainbows are a favorite target for all types of anglers. For bait fishermen, any combination of a worm and marshmallow is a likely bet.

Casting spinners and spoons also will catch lots of rainbows. There are dozens of different trout lures. Classics like Dardevle spoons, Rooster Tails, Panther Martin and Mepps spinners, Kastmasters and Super Dupers will consistently catch them.

Trolling is an excellent way to catch rainbows, either with a full trolling rig or lures. Rapalas and flatfish plugs also are good for trolling for rainbows.

Fly anglers should always have a few reliable rainbow favorites in their fly boxes. Elk hair caddis, woolly buggers, Parachute Adams, yellow- or cream-colored mayfly imitations, and classic nymphs like pheasant tails, prince nymphs and hare's ear work well.

### Good rainbow spots

South Fork of the Boise River, Lake Cascade, Lake Billy Shaw, Mountain View Reservoir, Horsethief Reservoir, Big Wood River, Silver Creek.

Cutthroat trout

## CUTTHROAT TROUT

This species derives its name from the brilliant orange slashes at the base of its gill plates. Cutthroats are close cousins to rainbow trout and they can interbreed, which has hurt some of Idaho's native populations.

In headwaters or desert rivers, this species might grow to only 8 inches and weigh less than a pound, while the largest cutthroat caught in Idaho tipped the scales at 18 pounds.

They are found in rivers and lakes, but you're more likely to find native cutthroat in rivers. They are stocked in mountain lakes because they are hardy fish that survive long winters and can grow with limited nutrients.

Cutthroat are considered the most gullible of all trout — a reputation that has been quantified by biologists. Scientists learned that cutthroats' aggressive nature also makes them susceptible to overharvest. Because of that, many cutthroat streams are catch and release, or have a small bag limit.

Cutthroats often are underappreciated because many anglers consider them second-class citizens compared to more-acrobatic rainbows.

### Cutthroat tactics

Dry flies are a great way to catch cutthroat because they will readily take them off the surface and add an exciting visual element to your fishing.

Cutthroat also will take wet flies and lures. Cutthroat like fast-moving water, so fish for them in riffles. It's counterintuitive because they are so colorful, but they have excellent natural camouflage and are almost impossible to see in the water until they chase your fly your lure.

In mountain lakes stocked with cutthroat, you can find them cruising the shallows in weed beds or around lily pads.

While cutthroat will take bait, it's illegal in some waters. Even where it's legal, if you plan to release cutthroat you should avoid bait. A fish could swallow the bait and make hook removal difficult without hurting the fish.

### Good cutthroat spots

Salmon River tributaries, upper stretches of the Boise River tributaries.

## BROWN TROUT

Brown trout are not native to North America, but they've been stocked here for more than a century. In 1880, brown trout eggs were first imported from Germany. In subsequent years, more eggs arrived from Scotland and England, which provided the brood stock for rivers and streams in the East. Stocking eventually moved west, and in many cases established self-sustaining brown-trout populations that continue today.

In Idaho, brown and rainbow trout have replaced native cutthroats in many streams, and the browns and rainbows thrive in the same waters.

Brown trout

9

Browns often grow larger than other trout in similar waters because they become piscivorous, which means they eat other fish. Their diet changes midway through their life cycle as more of their diet is based on other fish, which allows them to grow very large. The state record is 27 pounds.

Browns can be difficult to catch, which leads many anglers to believe the fish are smarter than other trout, but much of that difficulty lies in browns' habits rather than their intellect.

They are commonly taken with bait while they are actively feeding. Lures and flies will also catch them, but the challenge is getting to the fish. Brown trout favor heavy cover, and it's often difficult to coax them out of it.

Another biological factor in their favor is their vision. Because they live in dense cover, they see better in dim light and have more acute vision, which means they're better at spotting the difference between a fake offering and real food.

In heavily pressured waters, browns will feed early and late in the day or even at night to avoid disruptive anglers.

Adding to those challenges is the fact that browns eat mostly other fish when they reach 4 to 5 years old.

Browns can become almost bass-like in the way they lurk in heavy cover and ambush other fish.

Invade their space with a big streamer or lure and they likely will strike it. But you may end up losing a few lures or flies when they get tangled in the heavy cover.

Brown trout are good fighters, though not nearly as acrobatic as rainbows. Larger fish can be a real challenge because they often dart out of their lair and grab your fly or lure then make a mad dash back to the log, root wad, undercut bank or other obstacle.

### Brown trout tactics

Browns often fall prey to simple bait, like a worm drifted across the bottom. They will attack a spinner if it gets near them, especially in late summer and fall near their spawning season.

Browns are susceptible to streamer flies, and can't seem to resist a well-cast hopper pattern drifted near their hideout. Browns can also fall prey when they are rising to the surface to feed during insect hatches.

### Good brown trout spots

Owyhee River, Silver Creek, Big Wood River, Magic Reservoir, Horsethief Reservoir.

Brook trout

## BROOK TROUT

These are members of the char family, a closely related cousin to trout that shares many of the same physical features, habitat and habits as trout. Char generally live in very cold, clean water at high altitudes. Brook trout easily adapt to cool water where other trout thrive.

Brook trout are an interesting case study in the practice of stocking fish outside their native range. The native range of brook trout was once the area surrounding the Great Lakes and north into the eastern half of Canada and down through the mountains of the eastern U.S. all the way into northern Georgia.

Brook trout's native range has shrunk, and in waters where they once thrived, you will find non-native brown and rainbow trout.

But while their native range has gotten smaller, their introduced range, which includes Idaho, has significantly grown. Like brown trout and rainbow trout, brook trout are now part of the landscape.

Brook trout are small, plentiful and prolific breeders. The fish inhabit lakes and streams and can reproduce in both places.

Brook trout will readily take a fly, lure or bait, and are second only to cutthroat in their gullibility. But unlike cutthroat, which are prone to overharvest, brook trout are such prolific breeders that it's difficult to dent their populations through angling.

When too many fish inhabit a lake or stream, the result is an overabundance of undersized, malnourished fish. It's common in some small streams and mountain lakes to catch a brook trout on every cast, but none of the fish exceed 6 or 7 inches.

While some anglers rate brook trout barely above a nuisance, they can be an enjoyable game fish and a great way to introduce beginners to fishing.

### Brook trout tactics

You will rarely find a selective brook trout, which makes them fun quarry. Bring your lightest fishing tackle to enhance the fun of catching them.

### Good brook trout spots

Mountain lakes around McCall.

## GOLDEN TROUT

This species is indigenous to the Sierra Nevada Mountains in California and is the state fish, but it has been sporadically transplanted into mountain lakes in Idaho.

The golden trout has gold sides with red horizontal bands and dark markings. Goldens typically range from 6 to 12 inches.

The scarcity of golden trout means they aren't easy to find. Anglers who travel to mountain lakes where they are stocked will appreciate these beautiful fish and the pristine waters where they live.

### Golden trout tactics

There are no special tactics for targeting golden trout. Whatever works in mountain lakes will catch goldens. The fishing pressure is typically light in these lakes, and the growing season is short, so fish tend to be pretty aggressive.

### Good golden trout spots

To find the mountain lakes where they're being stocked check the current reports at www.fishandgame.idaho.gov.

## BULL TROUT

Bull trout are listed under the Endangered Species Act, so they cannot be harvested in Idaho.

So why should you care about them? Because you might catch one. But remember, bull trout must be immediately released unharmed.

Bull trout are mostly found in upper tributaries where they can find cold, clean water. They're pale to

Bull trout

dark olive and have white- pink- and salmon-colored spots. They resemble a brook trout, but an easy way to tell the difference is bull trout have no black on their fins.

Their diet mostly consists of other fish, but they will take bait, lures and flies.

## LAKE TROUT

This is a non-native member of the char family that has been transplanted into Idaho's large, deep lakes.

Catching lake trout typically requires special gear, like downriggers or leadcore trolling line. Catching one also takes good timing. Lake trout live deep where it's hard to get your gear to them, but in the spring they move into relatively shallow water and become more vulnerable to conventional tackle.

Lake trout are the largest of any char, trout or salmon species in Idaho. The state record is 57 pounds, which is bigger than even the largest chinook salmon ever caught in Idaho.

### Lake trout tactics
Troll with downriggers in deep-water lakes.

### Good lake trout spots
Payette Lake, Warm Lake, Stanley Lake.

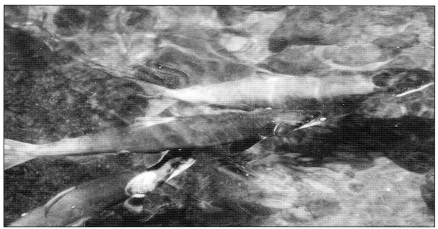
Kokanee salmon

## KOKANEE SALMON
Kokanee are land-locked sockeye salmon that are found in large reservoirs that have reasonably cool water year-round. Although landlocked, their life cycle mimics that of their ocean-going cousins.

They have short life spans, usually about three or four years. Kokanee are born in streams (or hatcheries) and descend into lakes and reservoirs to feed on plankton. As adults, they return to their spawning grounds in late summer and early fall. They undergo a dramatic physical change when they prepare to spawn. They go from a sleek, silvery salmon to a hook-snouted, humpbacked, red-bodied spawner.

Most angling occurs during spring and summer when kokanee are feeding in reservoirs.

### Kokanee tactics
Troll using deep-water tactics such as leadcore line or downriggers. Kokanee can be caught with bait such as maggots, mealworms or shoepeg corn.

### Good kokanee spots
Lucky Peak Reservoir, Deadwood Reservoir, Anderson Ranch Reservoir.

Steelhead

## STEELHEAD

Steelhead are large, sea-run rainbow trout that swim from Idaho's streams (and hatcheries) to the Pacific ocean then return from one to three years later. They swim all the way to the upper Salmon River near Stanley, a one-way trek of nearly 900 miles.

Steelhead range in size from a few pounds to a state-record 30 pounds, but most run in the 4- to 8-pound range. "B-run" fish, which typically spend two or more years at sea, range from 8 to 20 pounds.

Treasure Valley anglers typically fish for them in the Salmon and Snake rivers, and Fish and Game often brings truckloads of the fish to the Boise River in November.

Steelhead return to Idaho in late summer and fall with enough stored fat to carry them through the winter and into the spring spawning season.

They do not have to feed to survive, which makes them notoriously fickle. No one knows for sure why a steelhead strikes a fly, lure or bait, but we're all glad that they do.

They are large, hard-fighting fish that provide a long fishing season, typically from September through April. They're also accessible to bank and boat anglers.

### Steelhead tactics

For boat anglers, pulling plugs (working a boat against the current and trailing a lure downstream) and drifting bait (shrimp or salmon roe) are among the most popular methods.

Shore anglers hook them with lures and flies in the early season, then switch to bait or bobbers and jigs when the water gets cold.

In the spring, it's often bait or flies that catch steelhead as they move into the tributaries and headwaters for their spawning season.

Idaho anglers can keep only hatchery steelhead, which are identified by a clipped adipose fin, which is the small fin on the fish's back behind the dorsal fin.

### Good steelhead spots
Salmon River, Little Salmon River, Snake River below Hells Canyon Dam, Boise River.

## CHINOOK SALMON
In the past decade Idaho has experienced a resurgence of salmon fishing as larger runs have returned to Idaho.

Chinook salmon

Like steelhead, only hatchery chinook can be harvested by anglers. Like steelhead, you can spot a hatchery fish by its clipped adipose fin. All chinook with a full adipose fin must be immediately released unharmed.

Chinook return in spring, summer and fall, but most fishing occurs in spring and early summer.

They are typically larger than steelhead, often averaging from 10 to 12 pounds, but there are "jack" salmon (juvenile males that return from the ocean after less than a year) that usually weigh only a few pounds.

### Chinook tactics
Anglers typically target chinook in upper rivers and tributaries. Drifting bait or casting lures is the most popular way to fish for them.

In larger rivers, such as the Salmon River or the Snake River in Hells Canyon, boat anglers pull plugs to entice them.

### Good chinook spots
Salmon River, Snake River, Little Salmon River near Riggins, South Fork of the Salmon River east of Cascade.

## WHITEFISH
Many people mistake whitefish as cousins to suckers and pikeminnows, but they are actually closely related to salmon and trout.

Mountain whitefish are native to Idaho rivers and lakes. They share similar habitats and have the same feeding habits as trout. They are also similar in their fighting ability, although they're not known to jump like a trout.

Whitefish remain active in frigid water, which makes them excellent quarry for winter fishing.

Some people like to smoke or pickle whitefish, but most people are content to catch and release them.

Whitefish are game fish, so if you catch one and don't plan to eat it, immediately release it unharmed. If you kill it and toss it back into the river or the brush you can be cited for wasting game.

### Whitefish tactics

Whitefish are common in rivers, and you can catch them in water moving at a moderate speed, often above or below riffles or in pocket water.

Whitefish will take a piece of worm or salmon egg drifted along the bottom. They are fond of insect larvae, which makes them great quarry for fly anglers who like to nymph fish. Whitefish also will take dry flies off the surface during bug hatches.

### Good whitefish spots

South Fork of the Boise River, Boise River.

Sturgeon

## STURGEON

Sturgeon need no superlatives. They are one of the largest freshwater fish in the world and the largest in North America. Big ones measure more than 10 feet long.

They are native to the Snake River and found in its reservoirs.

All sturgeon are protected from harvest and any caught in Idaho must be immediately released unharmed. But the fish still provide a popular sport fishery.

### Sturgeon tactics

They are taken on specialized tackle, which is obviously stout and capable of reeling in a fish that could weigh more than 100 pounds.

Sturgeon are taken with bait sunk to the bottom. It's a waiting game, but when fishing is good, expect to catch ones in the 5- to 7-foot range. Whoppers are in the 9- to 10-foot range.

### Good sturgeon spots

Hells Canyon, C.J. Strike Reservoir, Snake River downstream from Bliss Dam.

# Warmwater fish

Smallmouth bass

Warmwater fish are popular in Southwest Idaho because they are readily available and have self-sustaining populations. Despite the warmwater name, these fish are catchable year-round and are found in a variety of waters.

## BASS

Idaho has largemouth and smallmouth bass, with smallmouths being the most common.

Largemouths are most often found in lakes, reservoirs and ponds. Smallmouths are commonly found in rivers and reservoirs, especially the Snake River and its reservoirs.

Smallmouths are typically the smaller of the two, but the size of the state records for each species are similar. The record smallmouth is just shy of 10 pounds, and the record largemouth almost 11 pounds.

Nick Young of Nampa is a professional bass angler who spends — and wins — thousands of dollars pursuing bass year-round in local, regional and national tournaments.

He said smallmouths prefer rocky areas — concrete dams, breakwaters and bridge abutments, gravel bars and underwater drop-offs — known as structure. You usually won't find them on sandy or muddy bottoms.

Smallmouths prefer cooler water and can live in moderate river currents. They also tend to be more mobile than largemouths.

Largemouths are more likely to be found in cover, which is typically some kind of vegetation such as weed beds, lily pads or submerged trees or brush.

Largemouths can tolerate warmer water, but do not like intense or direct sunlight. They like to ambush prey and typically don't roam as far as smallmouths except for seasonal migrations.

## Bass tactics

Bass fishing is not a passive activity. You don't cast a worm, let it sit and wait for something to happen. You might catch an occasional bass that way, but you're better off actively fishing for them.

"When you fish for bass, you're hunting," Young said.

There are many ways, but the most common method is to use lures, which are typically called baits in the bassing world.

## Action baits

Action baits such as spinnerbaits, crankbaits or jerkbaits are lures that are cast and retrieved and usually create lots of commotion in the water. For example, a topwater plug might resemble bass prey, but it's the action of the lure that usually attracts fish. Action baits often are best used early and late in the day.

Young encourages anglers to experiment with different retrieval speeds until they figure out what speed fish like on a particular day.

## Plastics

These baits typically are close imitations of natural bass foods, such as worms, leeches, minnows, crawdads or salamanders.

"The whole appeal of plastics is their realistic features," Young said.

The key to fishing plastics is getting them where the fish are, such as down in the rocks and weeds.

"As a rule of thumb, 80 percent of the time I try to keep my bait in contact with the cover or the structure I am fishing," Young said.

Instead of casting and retrieving, make your bait act like the creature it imitates.

"To catch the big boys and girls, you've got to make it look as realistic as possible," he said.

There are many ways to attach plastics, such as using a Texas rig, Carolina rig or drop-shotting. The different rigging techniques can seem overwhelming, but don't let them confuse you.

"Don't try to take it in all at once," Young said. "Learn one technique at a time."

He recommends drop-shotting as an excellent starting point, which is a fairly simple rig in which the bait is suspended on the line above a weight.

## Catching your first bass

Find tackle that gives you confidence, and regardless of what technique you use, pay attention to the details.

After you catch the first one, remember exactly what you were doing and start looking for clues and patterns that will help you determine the fishes' location and behavior.

"That first fish tells me a ton, and the next fish tells me even more," he said.

## Consider the seasons and conditions

Bass behave differently depending on the season.

In summer, bass avoid intense sun, so low-light conditions are the most productive, Young said.

The season also can help you determine where to go. Small ponds and lakes often get hot and choked with weeds during the summer, so you might try them in spring before the weeds start growing and try other areas until fall when the weeds break down.

Largemouth bass

### Good bass spots

**Brownlee Reservoir:** This is one of the top smallmouth destinations in the state. It's a large reservoir best fished from a boat, but some shore fishing is available. It also has largemouths.

**Snake River:** It's a good place for shore angling for smallmouths, but you have to move around to find prime spots.

**C.J. Strike Reservoir:** This large reservoir is famous for its smallmouths, but it also has largemouths. It's best for boat anglers, but there's plenty of shore access.

**Lake Lowell:** A great place for largemouths. Expect to fish in heavy cover in the summer when aquatic vegetation is in full bloom. If you don't have a boat, try fishing near the dam.

**Lake Cascade:** This is becoming a popular place for smallmouths, especially in the spring and early summer.

**Bruneau Dunes Lake and Crane Falls Reservoir:** These two bodies of water near Bruneau have largemouth bass and are good for small boats and float tubes. They also have places to fish from shore.

**Treasure Valley ponds:** They contain surprisingly good populations of largemouth bass, but are heavily pressured. You will have to work to catch fish, but they are there.

## CRAPPIE

Crappie are the largest of the "panfish" and Idaho has abundant populations of black and white varieties. The state record white and black crappie are more than 3 pounds.

---

Crappie

They are typically found in medium to large lakes and reservoirs and occasionally in ponds.

Crappie tend to run in large schools and have cyclical populations. During a boom year, a reservoir can have a seemingly inexhaustible supply. A year later, there might only be a fraction of the population.

Crappie can provide nearly nonstop action when fishing is good, which makes them great quarry for young or inexperienced anglers. The best fishing is usually in the spring when they move into the shallows to spawn.

Crappie are excellent table fare and you need only about six hand-sized crappie to make a good meal for an average adult.

### Crappie tactics

They will aggressively take a jig or bait, so you don't need a lot of fishing skill.

Small feathered or rubber-skirted jigs work well with a weighted jig head. Jigs are inexpensive, so buy them in lots of different colors and color combinations because certain colors will work better on some days. You also can tip your jig with a small amount of bait, like a bit of worm or crappie "nibbles," which are pellets designed as crappie bait.

Crappie also have a strange appetite for crickets, which will often out-fish other baits by a wide margin.

If crappie are near the surface, fish for them with a bobber and bait or jig suspended underneath. If they are deeper, cast and count the seconds until you start retrieving so you know what depth the fish are holding and can return to that same depth.

Crappie have soft mouths, which means they often come unhooked. A lightweight spinning rod with a soft action will help you land crappie and enjoy their scrappy fighting ability.

### Good crappie spots

Brownlee Reservoir, Oxbow Reservoir, C.J. Strike Reservoir, Paddock Reservoir.

## BLUEGILL

This species is a young angler's best friend. Bluegill are plentiful, aggressive, easy to find and fun to catch.

Bluegill are in the sunfish family, which includes a variety of fish of similar shape, but in different colors and sizes.

Bluegill flourish in small ponds and medium to large reservoirs. They like cover, such as weed beds, docks, overhanging trees and brush. They often are found in shallow water near shore.

Spring is the prime time for bluegill, because like crappie that's when they move into the shallows to spawn.

### Bluegill tactics

Bluegill will repeatedly attack bait, a small jig, or a fly and they fight hard for their size. A palm-sized bluegill can put a respectable bend in a rod.

Bluegill will devour almost any small fly floating on the surface and will take small wet flies and nymphs.

They have small mouths, so use small hooks and let them take the bait before you set the hook. If you're consistently missing strikes, let them fully take the bait and hook themselves. A small piece of worm or similar bait will suffice. Don't over-bait your hook or bluegill will nibble it away without hooking themselves.

### Good bluegill spots

Local ponds, C.J. Strike Reservoir, Crane Falls Reservoir, Lake Lowell.

Bluegill

Yellow perch

## YELLOW PERCH

Perch are plentiful and among the best-tasting freshwater fish.

They're found in large reservoirs and are popular quarry for ice anglers. They're not known for their fighting ability, but more than make up for it in table quality.

Perch can usually be found near the bottom. Start fishing with a worm and slowly retrieve it or jig it along the bottom. Once you find a fish, stick with that spot. You might alternate baits to find out what the fish prefer.

Perch tend to move to different spots depending on the season, but are fairly predictable in their migrations. Where you find perch at a certain time of year or under certain water conditions, you'll likely find them again under the same conditions.

Perch are similar to crappie because they are short-lived fish that go through boom and bust cycles. They are a popular game fish, but they can be a nuisance when illegally stocked in the wrong waters.

If perch are released into waters ill-suited for them, they take over a lake or reservoir with under-sized and malnourished fish that are too small to eat and provide little or no sporting value.

When that occurs, Fish and Game has to drain or poison the reservoir — which wipes out all fish, not just perch — then restock it with fish that can live and thrive there.

### Perch tactics

Perch are taken mostly with bait, but will bite lures and jigs. Worms are the most common bait, but that's partially because they're readily available.

Many anglers use cutbait, which is a piece of perch fillet. They will catch their first perch with a worm or other bait, then fillet the fish and use it for bait.

Ice anglers seem to be more specialized when targeting perch. They will use small jigs known as Swedish pimples, meal worms and maggots.

### Good perch spots

Magic Reservoir, C.J. Strike Reservoir, Lake Cascade.

## CATFISH

Catfish are one of the most under-utilized fish in Southwest Idaho. They are large and plentiful and surprisingly fun to catch.

They are common in the Snake River and its reservoirs, and in recent years Fish and Game has stocked them in ponds around the Treasure Valley.

Channel catfish are most common, but you might find flathead catfish or bullheads.

Flatheads are among the largest fish in the state. The state record of 58 pounds was taken from Brownlee Reservoir, and the state record channel cat is 31 pounds.

Catfish typically have healthy populations because they can live up to 25 years and survive in water conditions that are lethal to other fish.

### Catfish tactics

The best catfish fishing is usually in the late spring and early summer when the fish are spawning and are found in large schools in fairly shallow water. They will aggressively take all kinds of bait, including chicken livers, manufactured or home-made catfish baits and nightcrawlers.

While many people mistake catfish for bottom-feeding scavengers, they are actually omnivorous and adept predators that specialize in finding their prey in low visibility, usually in murky water or at night.

Catfish remain active in even the warmest water temperatures. During the hottest months, it's common to find schools of catfish in riffles on the Snake River.

### Good catfish spots

Snake River, Lake Lowell, C.J. Strike (Bruneau Arm).

Catfish

## CARP

It's ironic that the interest in carp as a sport fish has come from fly anglers.

Fly fisherman long ago accepted catch-and-release fishing, which meant table fare was no longer an issue, so they started rethinking their attitudes toward so-called trash fish.

Carp are plentiful, large (the state record is 37 pounds), hard-fighting and a challenge to catch. But what really makes them interesting quarry is you can sight fish for them.

Carp may seem like pushovers because they're so common in places like park ponds, but they are wily, intelligent fish that can easily sniff out a fake offering.

Carp

That means you have to be on your game to hook them and prepared for a battle to land them.

### Carp tactics

There are two main ways to fish for carp. The first is to use bait techniques similar to what you would use for catfish. Sink or drift bait along the bottom and hope one grabs it.

But the most exciting is sight fishing with a fly rod. Use a woolly bugger, leech, caddis nymph, small crawdad pattern or other carp fly and search for fish in the shallows.

When you spot a school, look for feeders, which typically churn the bottom with their noses pointed down and their tails up.

Cast a few feet in front of a feeding fish and watch its reaction. You often won't feel the take as a carp hovers over your fly and inhales it, then spits it out when it realizes it's a fake. Set the hook when you either feel tension on your line or see the fish take the fly.

If you get a good hook set, you're in luck because carp are nearly incapable of dislodging a hook from their tough, rubbery mouths.

Be prepared for numerous hard runs and expect the carp to seek every avenue of escape available, especially weed beds and reeds.

### Good carp spots

Snake River, Lake Lowell, Boise ponds.

# Basic tackle

Anglers sometimes make fishing too complicated. Here's all you need to get started.

**Rod and reel:** Buy or borrow a medium-weight spinning rod. It'll catch everything from small crappie to whopper trout. Rod-and-reel packages start at about $40. You can get a kids' combination setup even cheaper.

**Reel and line:** If you don't get a rod and reel combination, a medium-weight spinning reel is good for all-around fishing. Don't buy the cheapest line. Spend a few extra dollars for a name-brand 4- to 8-pound test line, which is less prone to tangles.

**Tackle:** Buy hooks, split-shot weights and bobbers so you have the option to fish either on the top or the bottom of a lake, reservoir or pond.

**Bait:** Worms, salmon eggs, corn or PowerBait is the easiest setup for beginners. If you're fishing near the bottom, use a small marshmallow to float your worm.

**Fishing license:** Everyone 14 or older needs one. If you're helping a child cast or reel in, you need one, too. Licenses are available at Idaho Department of Fish and Game offices and most sporting goods stores. Free fishing day (no license required) is held each year in June. It's a great chance for beginners to try out the sport.

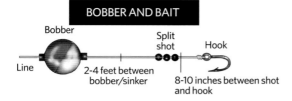

**BOBBER AND BAIT**

Bobber

Split shot

Hook

Line

2-4 feet between bobber/sinker

8-10 inches between shot and hook

## How to tie an improved cinch knot

**1** Run about 5 inches of line through the eye of the hook.

**2** Wrap the line from five to seven times back around itself.

**3** Run the loose end through the loop in the line near the eye of the hook, then back though larger loop you just made. Pull tight.

**WEIGHT AND BAIT**

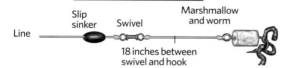

Slip sinker

Swivel

Marshmallow and worm

Line

18 inches between swivel and hook

### BOBBER AND BAIT RIG

This can catch bluegill, crappie, perch and trout.

➤ Clip a small, round bobber from 2 to 4 feet from the end of your line.

➤ Tie on a hook (size 6 through 12) at the end of the line below the bobber. You might add a small split-shot about 8-10 inches above the hook to sink your bait.

➤ The bobber can be moved up and down, depending on how deep the fish are. When you start getting fish, stay at that depth.

➤ Add a small worm to the hook, not a big piece of nightcrawler. Some fish are dainty when they take the bait.

➤ For trout, you can use a single salmon egg instead of a worm.

➤ For bluegill, bass, or trout you can try a cricket or grasshopper.

### BAIT AND SLIP SINKER RIG

A marshmallow-worm combo with a slip sinker, sometimes called an egg sinker, is one of the most common fishing rigs in Idaho. With this rig, fish can pick up the bait and swim with it without feeling the sinker. You will know a fish is taking the bait because your line will start running out.

You can substitute other bait like salmon eggs, corn, PowerBait or marshmallows. You also can use cheese baits that come in garlic and anise flavors. Trout like Velveeta cheese, too. Here's the basic rig:

➤ Cut an 18-inch piece of line off the main line on your fishing reel.

➤ Put a slip sinker on your main line. It's an oblong weight with a narrow hole through the center.

➤ Tie a small barrel swivel or snap swivel on the end of the line to keep the sinker from slipping off the line. At the other end of the swivel, tie on the 18 inches of loose line and a size 6 hook.

➤ The sinker can't go past the swivel, so when you cast it stays 18 inches above the hook. If you pull on the hook, the line slips through the sinker. You can pull 2 or 3 feet of line through the sinker.

➤ Bait the hook. Put a marshmallow on first and push it up to the eye of the hook.
➤ Put on a worm. The marshmallow keeps the worm off the bottom and makes it more attractive to fish.

## FISHING WITH KIDS
➤ Keep it simple with a worm-and-marshmallow rig or a bobber and worm.
➤ Choose a place where you know there are lots of fish. Local ponds are great places. Go to www.fishandgame.idaho.gov to get a recent stocking report. If fishing is slow and they get bored, it is a short drive home.

➤ If you have a canoe or small boat and can fish a small lake or reservoir, try trolling with a spinner like a Mepps, Panther Martin or Rooster Tail. As you paddle along with the lines out, the trout hook themselves. It is a simple way for kids to catch fish and enjoy a boat ride.

➤ If the kids are very young, take their favorite toys. They may just want to run their toy trucks in the mud. Go with the flow. If you are fishing from the bank of a sandy reservoir, take a shovel and bucket and build sand castles. No sand? Skip rocks or throw flat pieces of driftwood into the water.

➤ Make sure kids are dressed for the weather. You may be able to tough out bad weather, but they will be miserable and end up hating fishing and never want to go again.

➤ Take along snacks and other goodies. Small anglers travel on their stomachs.

➤ Treat them to lunch or dinner at their favorite place after a trip. If you're going early in the morning, stop for breakfast. They'll associate fishing with blueberry pancakes.

# Bait fishing

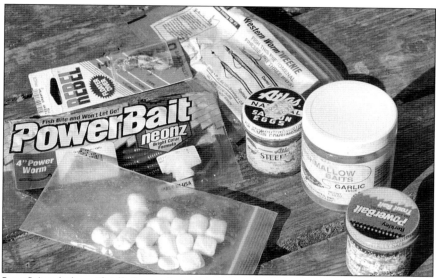

PowerBait and other artificial baits come in a variety of shapes and flavors.

Say bait fishing and the first image that comes to mind is a forked stick, a line and a worm. There's nothing wrong with keeping fishing simple, but there are a lot of options for bait.

## Worms

This probably is the most versatile bait known to man. Worms will catch almost any fish — from bluegill to sturgeon. Most people use nightcrawlers, but any earthworm will do. A small piece often will work as well as a big glob, depending on the species you're targeting.

## Salmon eggs

These have long been a popular trout bait. Salmon roe (clusters of eggs) also is a popular bait for steelhead and chinook salmon.

## PowerBait and other artificial bait

PowerBait is popular for trout and occasionally other species. Artificial baits are made of resin, so they're good for beginners because there isn't the squirm factor of impaling a live worm. PowerBait also floats, so it gets your bait above the weeds in a pond or reservoir.

Some artificial baits mimic worms or maggots.

Berkely Gulp baits have the scent and lifelike feel of the things they imitate, which can be anything from worms and shrimp to minnows and maggots. Some are designed for a particular fish, such as "Crappie Nibbles."

### Grasshoppers and crickets

These are some of the most fun baits to fish, especially in rivers during the summer because you get to see trout take them off the surface. Crickets are good for bluegill, bass and crappie. Unlike grasshoppers, they are available at bait shops so you don't have to catch your own.

### Minnows

It is illegal to use live fish for bait in Idaho, but dead minnows are allowed. Minnows can be effective for warmwater fish like bass and catfish.

### Mealworms and maggots

Once you get past the gross-out factor, they are good for ice fishing, particularly for perch. Maggots are also used for kokanee bait.

### Catfish baits

There are hundreds of recipes for these smelly pastes that catfish like. You can make your own using anything from chicken livers to cheese.

### Crawdads

They make good bait for bass and trout. If you're using them for trout, peel the meat out of the tail and put it on your hook. You can legally use live crawdads, but only if you catch them from the same body of water you are fishing.

### Corn

No one seems to know why, but trout like corn and kokanee salmon seem to have a particular taste for shoepeg corn.

### Marshmallows

Small marshmallows are commonly paired with a worm or salmon eggs to float other bait off the bottom of a lake or reservoir. Marshmallows alone can catch a lot of trout, too. The hard part is keeping kids out of the bait.

## Shrimp

This is another strange bait, considering Idaho is hundreds of miles from the ocean. But shrimp are a popular bait for steelhead. Pink cocktail shrimp are often used by ice anglers to catch trout.

## Cutbait

Many perch anglers use the first fish they catch as bait. Fillet a small piece and dangle it from your hook. Jigging will often entice reticent perch to strike.

## BAIT FISHING TIPS

➤ Using a bobber and bait is often the best technique if fish are near the surface. It's also a great way to teach kids and beginners to fish because it's exciting when the bobber bounces and then disappears from the surface.

➤ Fish the fast, shallow riffles in a river. Trout will feed and hold in ankle-deep water. You have to pick a bait rig that's heavy enough to cast, but light enough to stay off the bottom. Cast directly across the stream and let your lure swing through the riffle.

➤ Make it look natural. Fish are like fine diners. They like their meal with a good presentation. If you're fishing a river, use only as much weight as you need to get it to the depth you're aiming for and let it drift naturally.

➤ In weedy water, float your bait above the weeds. You can do this with artificial bait that floats or by pairing your bait with a marshmallow.

➤ Drift a live grasshopper without weight. This can be very effective in small rivers and streams. Leave your bail open and let the hopper drift downstream. When a fish swims to the surface and gulps the hopper, quickly spin the reel handle to flip the bail and set the hook.

➤ Don't be afraid to cast bait and retrieve, but do it slowly. You want to cover water, but still have it look fairly natural. Slowly casting and retrieving a worm

across the bottom can be irresistible for smallmouth bass, and the sound of the weight hitting on the rocks is an additional attraction.

➤ Don't overload your hook with bait. A smaller piece of bait will usually attract as many fish and result in more hook-ups.

➤ Experiment. Some days fish might take a bait that is sitting still; other times they might like jigging (a jerking motion) or slow, steady retrieves. If you're not catching anything, try a different method.

# Spinners & spoons

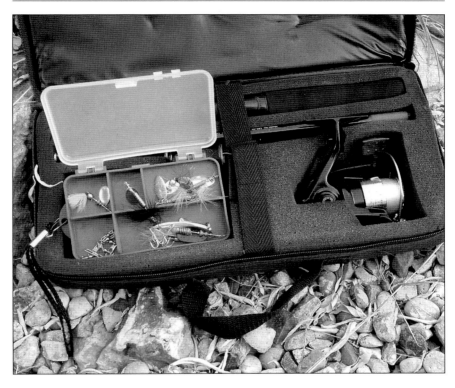

We were going to write our own section, but realized the best advice already existed. This is an abridged version of a Luhr Jensen tech report. The company's publications provide excellent information for all types of fishing.

## RULE NO. 1: MIX IT UP

Do everything you can to prevent a lure from running at a constant speed and in a straight line. Twitch the rod tip every few seconds. Speed up and then slow down the retrieve. Stop the lure dead in the water and start it up again. Reel extremely fast for a few seconds. The more variety in speed and action you impart on the lure, the better your chances of enticing a strike.

## MASTER A LURE'S ACTION

Another important thing to know is the feel and action of a lure under a variety of water conditions.

A clear lake or pond, or a quiet, deep hole in a river are excellent spots to watch the action of a lure in relation to rod vibration. An angler with a solid understanding of a lure's vibration and action can, by watching the rod tip, determine the necessary retrieve speed and judge whether or not the lure is working properly.

Start by making a short cast and then begin a slow, steady retrieve, constantly keeping your eyes on your rod tip. A vibrating tip means the spoon or spinner is working. As the lure approaches you, watch what it is doing underwater and couple that with the rod tip vibrations and the "feel" you are getting.

A spoon should swim with a side-to-side wobble, while a spinner should have a constantly revolving blade. If your spoon is spinning, you are reeling too fast.

If the blade on your spinner is not constantly revolving, you are reeling too slowly.

Spinners

Spoons

### SPINNERS VS. SPOONS

Spoons' actions are determined by their shape. Generally, the longer a spoon is in relation to its width, the tighter it will wobble and the more retrieve speed or river current it will tolerate.

All spinners produce sonic vibrations under water. Some produce more than others depending on the shape of the blade and how it is attached to the shaft.

### TIPS FOR SPINNERS AND SPOONS

➤ Most anglers try to fish spinners too quickly, even though the most effective method is a slow-moving lure fished near the bottom.

➤ A barrel or snap swivel needs to be attached to the eye of the lure to prevent line twist.

➤ A spoon should be attached to your line with a rounded attachment device, whether it's a welded ring, split ring or snap. Sharply pointed or V-shaped snaps or snap swivels ruin the action of most spoons.

➤ If fish appear finicky (they follow the lure but won't strike it) your line might be too visible. Switch to a smaller-diameter line or a flourocarbon leader, which is less visible under water.

➤ Lure finishes are best chosen according to the weather conditions. On dark days or at periods of low light, such as early morning or late afternoon, a brass or copper finish will work well. On bright days or in clear water, choose nickel finishes. Brass or copper work well when water is brackish, murky or deep.

➤ Select your spoons based on the depth you want to fish. Narrow, longer spoons generate less water resistance and sink faster than wider spoons, especially in strong river currents. Wide spoons generate more water resistance, which keeps them running shallower.

## SPINNERS IN RIVERS

Spinners can be effective in rivers by casting upstream, cross-stream and downstream.

With spinners with wide blades, the upstream technique can be particularly deadly and is best accomplished with a high-speed spinning reel.

Cast the spinner and immediately begin reeling to start the blade in motion. As soon as the blade begins turning, you will see and feel vibration in the rod tip.

If you feel steady ticks from a spinner blade, the lure is too close to the bottom and you should reel faster.

If you don't feel a tap once in a while, slow down because the lure isn't working close enough to the bottom. You should use a retrieve speed that causes the spinner blade to nick a rock or touch bottom every few seconds.

## SPOONS IN RIVERS

When fishing spoons, the most common cast will be straight across the stream or just slightly upstream, allowing the spoon to sink a moment or two before beginning a retrieve. As the spoon works downstream and catches the current, you should slow your retrieve.

As it works across the stream toward your position, stop reeling. Once the lure has reached quiet, soft water and has begun to settle toward the bottom (vibrations at the rod tip will fade), it's time to slowly reel in and make another cast.

Tailout areas are popular spots for feeding, resting and holding fish. These areas are at the end of a hole or drift where the water shallows and picks up speed. Because they're shallow, tailouts are hard to fish with cross-stream casts and are best covered with downstream casts.

Position yourself above the tailout and cast across and downstream. When the spoon or spinner hits the water, take a few turns of your reel handle and then let the current do the rest of the work, pushing and activating the lure as it crosses the river back to your bank.

## LAKE FISHING

In lake fishing with either spoons or spinners, fish will be found at different levels depending on the location of food sources, the time of day, the degree of sunlight and the water temperature.

River fish, on the other hand, generally tend to be found close to the bottom unless a major insect hatch draws them to the surface.

If casting a spoon or a spinner into a lake, you should try to vary the depth of each retrieve until you find where the fish are holding. Mentally mark that depth so you can go back to it on the next cast.

A standard quarter-ounce spoon or spinner on a tight line (they sink faster on a slack line) will sink about one foot per second. You can count the number of seconds it takes to reach bottom (the line goes slack) and then make your first retrieve slow and close to the bottom.

On each successive cast, subtract two seconds of sinking time until you have covered every foot of depth in a particular area.

Used with permission from Luhr Jensen/Rapala. Get more fishing advice at www.luhrjensen.com/tech-info/tech-reports.

# Trolling tips

Trolling is a popular way to fish lakes and reservoirs because you can cover a lot of water to find fish. It's about the only way you can consistently catch kokanee salmon in Southwest Idaho. Trollers often take some of the largest trout out of reservoirs because they can get to the depths where those big fish lie.

Trolling can be as simple as pulling a spinner, spoon or plug, like a Flatfish or Rapala, behind a canoe or rowboat. With a bigger investment in gear you can use trolling rigs, electronic fish finders, downriggers or leadcore line.

Whatever method you choose, a few tips can make your trolling efforts more successful. We turned to Mike Boxberger at Tackle Tom's in Cascade, a trolling specialist, for advice. He can consistently take large trout from notoriously fickle Lake Cascade. The skills he uses can be successful in other waters.

## TROLLING TIPS

➤ Use colored leadcore line instead of monofilament line. Leadcore line is specifically designed for trollers. It has a different color every 10 yards and sinks from 4 to 5 feet per color. You can control the depth of your tackle by how much line you let out and easily identify the depths by the different colors.

➤ Use a trolling rig. There are a variety of them on the market — Cow Bells, Beer Cans, Doc Shelton and Ford Fenders — that come in a variety of sizes, shapes and colors. Check local tackle shops to get a recommendation for a good one to start with, then buy a few more and experiment until you find one that works.

➤ Trail a Wedding Ring spinner and bait from 12 to 18 inches behind your trolling rig.

➤ Don't put a big glob of worm on your hook. A little piece will hook more fish.

➤ For kokanee salmon, use a snubber, which is a piece of rubber that absorbs the shock when a fish hits. Kokanee have soft mouths and a hook can easily tear out.

➤ During summer, fish below the thermocline, which is usually from 15 to 20 feet down. It's the cooler water, which has a higher oxygen content and is better for fish.

➤ In general, trolling slowly is best. Troll about 1 mph. If you don't have a speedometer, that's about the speed of a slow walk.

➤ Steer the boat in a serpentine course. It covers more water, varies the speed of your trolling rig and makes it abruptly change direction. Fish will sometimes follow a trolling rig, but not strike. A sudden change in direction, however, can trigger a strike.

➤ If you're losing lots of fish after the initial strike, try a stiffer rod and the fish likely will hook themselves.

➤ Use a fish finder, but be skeptical of what you see — or don't see. It might be showing trash fish rather than game fish. Fish finders also don't pick up all fish. Pay particular attention to the depth where you're seeing fish and make sure your gear is there.

➤ If you don't have a fish finder, remember that fish tend to be in schools. If you have a strike or catch a fish, troll back through that same area.

➤ If you're trolling with a spinner in a small reservoir or lake, you're usually

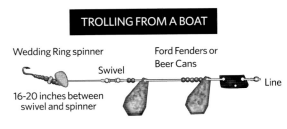

### TROLLING FROM A BOAT

Wedding Ring spinner

Ford Fenders or Beer Cans

Swivel

Line

16-20 inches between swivel and spinner

better off fishing close to shore near natural land features like points and cliffs. That's where fish are likely to congregate. Start near the edges and then work your way into deep water.

# Fly fishing gear basics

I t seems like there's been an arm's race in the fly fishing industry to see who can make the most expensive equipment and the most gadgets and attire to carry it all. It's gotten to the point that the presumed "must-haves" for fly fishing cost as much as a mortgage payment. It's not all frivolous. But you don't need much to get started — an 8- or 9-foot five-weight graphite fly rod, a reel, a fly line, a leader and a few flies — will do. You eventually may want to invest in the bells and whistles, but don't let it be a hurdle for getting into the sport. The Statesman's Roger Phillips, a lifelong fly fisherman (and self-confessed gear junkie), will help you make smart choices.

## THE ROD: WHY A FIVE WEIGHT?

Any fish from 6 inches long to 5 pounds is fair game with a five weight. Some may quibble, but a palm-sized bluegill will give you a fair tussle on a five weight and the rod still has enough backbone to land a 24-inch trout.

Almost every manufacturer makes a reasonably priced five-weight rod, and you get to set your price. You could pay from $50 to $800.

Consider the five weight the dollar bill of fly fishing: It's the basic unit of currency. Rods go from zero weight to 20 weight. You can land a marlin or a giant tuna with a 20 weight. They're the upper end of what's possible to land on a fly rod. These days, there are few species of fish that haven't been caught with a fly rod.

So if you can land a bluegill on a five weight, what's a zero weight for? The gist of a zero weight is it's similar to an ultra-light spinning rod. It's designed to give you the maximum play out of a fish. A zero-weight rod would make a 12-inch rainbow trout feel like a marlin. A 16-inch trout probably could snap a zero-weight rod in half and hand it back to you.

There's another detail you should know: Rods come in different actions. If you've owned a few spinning rods, this isn't a new concept. The action of a fly rod is a little different, however, because of the way you cast it.

With a spinning rod, you whip the rod and let your lure fly. If you want to fling your lure farther, you add a little more weight and whip it a little harder.

Adding weight to change how far you can cast is not an option on a fly rod. For the most part, the combined weight of the line and fly will be fairly constant. Some flies are heavier than others, but even a heavy fly weighs about the same as a few feet of fly line. So the majority of weight will be in the line, which does not change.

Enter a fly rod's action.

## THE ROD: WHAT KIND OF ACTION?

Fly rods have either a slow, medium or fast action. With slow action, the rod flexes all the way to its butt during a cast, which is why some companies describe their rods as full flex, rather than slow action. With a fast-action rod, the top third or so flexes (tip flex) and a medium falls in between the two.

Rather than a technical explanation of how flex affects a cast, let's pretend we're tossing a ball instead of casting a fly. A slow-action rod is like arching a pitch in softball, and a fast-action rod is like pitching a baseball.

In both cases you're trying to get the ball over the plate, but with a fly rod you're trying to cast a fly to a given spot. With a slow-action rod, everything happens a little more slowly and, arguably, with a little more control. You have more time to react to what the rod is doing, which is flexing and storing energy then springing and releasing it.

With a fast-action rod, this occurs more quickly. Like pitching a fastball, you may have less control initially when you're learning to cast. Your timing has to be better to use a fast-action rod. The flip side is the rod will deliver your fly with more power after you get the hang of it.

So does that mean everyone eventually wants a fast-action rod? Not at all. Once you get the hang of casting, it becomes personal preference.

If you buy a $50 fly fishing package, you won't have a choice of action. But the more you pay for a fly rod, the more options you will have.

## THE ROD: HOW MUCH SHOULD YOU PAY?

There isn't a rule of thumb for how much you should pay for your first fly rod.

More expensive rods are usually better. But a $600 rod is not six times better than a $100 rod. It won't cast six times farther. It won't catch six times more fish. A top-shelf rod will be a joy to cast and a piece of equipment you can take pride in owning, but it's certainly not a necessity.

If you're the type of person who likes quality stuff, buy a mid-priced rod for your first one. If possible, cast it first. If it feels right to you, buy it, even if it's the cheapest rod on the rack. The goal is to find a rod that will keep you happy for many years.

Look for a rod company that offers a no-fault warranty. Fly rods can break easily, and the cost of replacing one under warranty is a lot cheaper than buying another one.

If you're more cost-conscious, buy a fly-fishing package. They're the best deal going. You're not going to be able to choose each component, but for between $100 and $200, you can get a rod, reel, line, backing and often an instructional video. You will save a few bucks, but you may end up replacing your gear within a year or two after you get more experience.

Even if that happens, don't sweat it. Say you paid $150 for a fly fishing package and got two years and a dozen fishing trips out of it before you upgraded. If you never used your beginner gear again it cost you $75 per year — or about $12.50 every time you used it. That's pretty cheap entertainment. You can always loan it to a buddy to help him or her get started or pass it on to your kids.

## REELS

You want a fly reel that matches your line size. Most reels will accommodate about three different line sizes. You can spend a little more and get a large arbor or a medium (or mid-arbor) reel. The arbor is the spool on the reel. The larger the arbor, the more line you retrieve with each turn of the handle. I like mid- and large-arbor reels, but I also fish a standard-arbor reel and have no real complaints, especially on a trout rod.

I think most fly reels are horribly overpriced. A fly reel is a simple mechanism. Turn the handle once, the arbor turns once. There's a mechanism to keep it from free-spooling, and most reels have a drag just like a spinning reel.

I once bought a fly reel for about $25. I used it to catch a whole mess of fish, including lots of trout (a few even measured in pounds rather than inches), some bass, bluegill, whitefish and a few species I usually don't admit in public that I

caught on a fly rod. I also lost a bunch of fish, but I can say with a straight face and a clear conscience that I never lost a fish because of my $25 reel. It did its job just fine.

I now own several beautiful, shiny and silky-smooth reels for my trout and steelhead rods. They're fine pieces of machinery and I have no regrets about buying them. But if someone who is just getting started asks me what to buy, I steer him or her toward an inexpensive reel.

## FLOATING LINE

Get a weight-forward, five-weight floating line to go with your five-weight rod.

Floating line is easiest to cast. It requires less force to pull it off the water because it's lighter than a sinking line. You can fish all types of flies — dries, wets, nymphs and streamers — with a floating line. But you can't fish dry flies with a sinking line.

Weight forward makes a floating line even easier to cast. Weight forward refers to the fly line's taper. Unlike monofilament line that is uniform in diameter, fly line is tapered at different places along its length. The thickest part of a weight-forward line is the front section. Since a heavier object has more momentum than a lighter one traveling at the same speed, the end of the fly line is going to shoot out farther and carry your fly with it.

## SINKING LINES

If you're fishing a lot of lakes, ponds and reservoirs, a sinking line is good to have.

There are obvious advantages. A sinking line will get the fly down to the fish.

There are a variety of sinking lines, including full-sinking and sink-tip lines in which only the end of the line sinks. There also are different sink rates, which are listed as Type I, II, III, etc. The larger the number the more quickly the line sinks.

The disadvantages of sinking lines are they are more difficult to cast and you are limited to wet flies, streamers and nymphs. You can always fish those with a floating line, you just won't get them as deep.

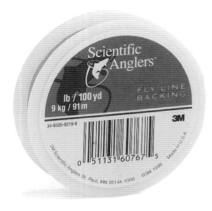

## BACKING

You will also want some braided Dacron backing — a length of line that attaches your casting line to your reel — which serves a couple purposes. If you're fishing with a standard-arbor reel, it will keep your fly line from getting tightly wrapped on your reel. You will also be able to retrieve your fly line more quickly because the backing increases the diameter of the spool.

Backing also is insurance against a big fish taking all of your fly line. Your five-weight line will be about 90 feet long, and your leader will be about 9 feet. That gives you about 99 feet of line to work with. Let's say you're casting 30 feet, which is a normal cast. That gives you 69 feet of line to work the fish with. If a fish takes a big run, it could take all your line. That's where the backing comes in. Rather than the end of the fly line tightening against your reel, the fish will start peeling off the backing, which is usually another couple hundred feet or so. If the fish takes all that, you're either headed to the fly-fishing hall of fame or you need to tighten your drag.

## LEADER

Remember the five-weight rod and five-weight line? Remember another five — 5X. That's the leader you want. It actually has nothing in common with five-weight line, which is matched to your rod. Leaders are tapered monofilament line, which means at the thick end (the butt) it's very heavy and strong (in the 20- to 30-pound test range). You don't need to worry about the butt, you need to worry about the tip.

Here's an annoying part of fly fishing. Somewhere back in time, fly leaders were measured by their diameter. Every other monofilament fishing line is rated by strength and stated as "pound test." But leaders are identified by a number followed by an "X." A 5X leader means the end of the tapered leader is 5X diameter, which is typically between 4- and 5-pound test, depending on the brand.

The larger the number before the "X," the lower the strength, or pound-test, the tip is. An 8X leader would be less than 2-pound test. A 1X tippet would be about 10-pound test. You can use any size of leader with your fly line. Typically, you match the leader with the fly, but you also have to consider the size of the fish you are likely to catch. That's why 5X is a good starting point. It will work with most flies and most trout.

Leaders also come in different lengths, usually from 7½ to 12 feet. Nine-foot leaders are the standard. So remember, 9-foot, 5X leader. You may want to start with a shorter leader. It will make casting a little easier and shorter leaders are less likely to tangle into wind knots, the bane of all fly casters.

### TIPPETS

Tippets basically are an extension of your leader. They also come in "X" sizes. There are two reasons for a tippet. First, leaders are expensive. A good leader will cost about $3.

In the course of tying on flies and cutting or breaking them off, your leader will get shorter and larger in diameter because it's tapered. You can tie tippet onto your leader to extend it back to its original length. A spool with 30 feet of 5X tippet will cost about $4. A 9-foot leader is about $3. It's a lot cheaper to tie on a couple feet of tippet than to replace the whole leader.

The second reason for tippets is to accommodate different sizes of flies. If you are trying to tie a size 20 fly on a 5X leader, the line may be too thick to fit through the eye of the hook. Rather than replacing a 5X leader with a 6X or 7X, you can tie a couple feet of smaller tippet onto a 5X leader.

### WADERS

In most cases, fly fishing requires room for a backcast, which can be tough if you're standing with your back to shore. The easiest way to get room for a backcast when you're river fishing is to wade. It's also a good way to get closer to the prime fishing spots.

So waders are a necessity, right? Not at all. If you fish only during the summer, you can throw on a pair of quick-drying shorts, an old pair of tennis shoes or sandals and go fishing.

As soon as the water is warm enough to go without waders, I am out there in shorts and wading boots and enjoying every minute of it.

But eventually you will want waders, either neoprene or a pair made out of waterproof, breathable fabric.

Neoprene waders will keep you very warm in cold water. That can also work against you in the summer. They can be sweltering hot. If you're thinking, "Who cares, I can wade in shorts during the summer," be warned: A lot of rivers fed by reservoirs behind dams are frigid, even in the summer. If you like early-morning fishing, it can get pretty chilly.

Waterproof/breathable waders are the latest, greatest thing, and they work well. Many people call them Gore-Tex waders, which is a brand name that has become synonymous with waterproof/breathable fabric, but other companies make similar versions. The price for the fabric has dropped dramatically in recent years, but they're still more expensive than neoprene waders.

The advantage of fabric waders is that they are much lighter and more comfortable. They breathe, which lets moisture escape and prevents you from getting clammy when you sweat. On cold days or in cold water, you can layer more clothes under them to make them warmer.

Aside from being more expensive, fabric waders are more prone to punctures and scrapes — which means leaks — unless you buy really expensive models. With reasonable care, though, even a modestly priced pair should last a couple seasons. There are repair kits available to patch leaks.

Finally, you will have the option of stocking-foot waders or waders with boots attached. Boot waders are more expensive, but generally cheaper than buying wading boots and waders separately. But the attached boots won't fit as snugly or provide as much ankle support as wading boots.

You're also likely to wear out waders faster than your boots, but if the boots are attached, you're going to be throwing them out with your waders. If you buy wading boots separately they can last through several sets of waders.

## WADING BOOTS

Wading boots usually come with felt soles, which grip rocks like Velcro. If you pay more, you can get felt soles with cleats, which provide even better traction.

Some companies are moving away from felt soles because they can transport unwanted organisms between bodies of water. The high-traction rubber soles provide similar traction to felt and are more convenient because they retain less water and dry more quickly.

## FLY BOX

Sometimes when you get too cheap, it ends up costing you more. I learned this lesson with fly boxes. I didn't want to spend $10 on a fly box, so I bought a clear plastic box for about a dollar at discount store and put my flies in it. It worked fine until I was wading in a river and dropped it with the lid open. All my flies floated downriver. The cost to replace them was much

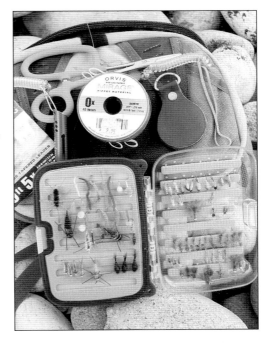

more than the cost of a real fly box. There are lots of boxes out there for a wide range of prices. Make sure they hold individual flies securely or in small compartments with separate lids.

## CLIPPERS

These are extremely handy. You can buy them at a fly shop for $5 to $10, or get fingernail clippers at a drug store for 69 cents. You make the call.

## FLY FLOATANT

If you're fishing with dry flies — and you will definitely want to because it's the most fun and exciting way to fly fish — floatant will keep your fly from being waterlogged. This spray-on substance costs a few bucks, and since you use it so sparingly (it doesn't take much to coat a fly), it will last a long time. Consider it a must-have.

## NET

You can easily land a trout by hand. You don't even have to take it out of the water. Land the fish, hold it gently in your hand, grab the fly and give it a quick backward jerk (barbless flies make it much easier on you and the fish), and the fish is back on its way. If you want a net, you can get by with a cheap one for a few bucks at any sporting goods store. I prefer an oval-shaped net with fine mesh. They're commonly known as "catch-and-release nets." The fine mesh is easier on the fish and the nets don't get hung up in the brush nearly as much as regular nets. I justify spending the extra money because I think it benefits the fish, not me.

## FORCEPS

This is another item that benefits the fish. Grab the hook's shank with these plier-like gizmos and you have excellent leverage to remove a hook.

## LEADER STRAIGHTENER

This is optional, but it's also inexpensive, durable and will make your life easier, so go ahead and buy one. Monofilament leaders have "memory," which means when you unwind them, they look like a corkscrew. Run it through a leader straightener and the line straightens out. A straight leader gives your fly a better presentation. It makes life easier, improves your fishing and cost less than $5.

## FLY VEST OR CHEST PACK

You will quickly find that your fly box and gadgets won't fit in pants and shirt pockets, so you need some place to put them. Fly vests were the longtime favorite, but chest packs have gained popularity. Both work well and it comes down to personal preference.

Make sure whatever you use is comfortable. It's surprising how much pressure a vest with a few pounds of gear can exert on you. If you feel a burning pain in your neck or between your shoulders after a couple hours of fishing, your vest could be the culprit. If you tend to be a pack rat, make sure your vest or pack can comfortably carry the load.

## OTHER GADGETS

There are a lot of them. Apparently fly fishermen love shiny little gadgets — space-age clippers, retractors, mini flashlights that clip to the brim of your hat and stomach pumps so you can see what a trout has been eating.

If you want to spend money on them, feel free. Just don't think you have to in order to catch fish. Fish don't care how many trinkets are hanging around your neck or stuffed into your fly vest. All they care about is a well-presented fly that resembles something they eat.

You can't spend your way to fishing success.

# Fly fishing tactics

Fly fishing was once seen as an archaic method of angling for people who chose tradition over technology. But things have changed. Modern fly rods and lines make it easy to learn to cast and flies are available in all styles — from traditional feathered patterns to those tied completely with synthetic materials.

The line between conventional tackle and fly tackle is blurring and catch rates by fly anglers are often on par with those who use conventional tackle. While fly fishing is most commonly associated with trout fishing, fly anglers target nearly all species and can successfully catch them.

Here's how they do it.

### DRY FLY FISHING

This is arguably the most exciting method because you get to watch a fish rise to pluck a fly off the surface. You'll use flies that imitate insects that are hatching off the water or "attractor" patterns that tempt fish to strike.

Dry flies typically are "dead drifted" on a slack line so they look like a bug drifting in the current. You can use them on lakes or ponds by letting them sit and wait for a fish to find them.

Parachute Adams

### Fill your fly box with ...

**Parachute Adams:** This imitates a lot of mayfly species, and in smaller sizes imitates midges. It's one of the most popular flies. Have a few in your box in different sizes.

**Royal Wulff:** This is a variation of a classic attractor pattern with tufts of calf hair for wings. It's an excellent pattern in large and small sizes.

**Stimulator:** It's a good attractor pattern, especially for rivers. Large sizes imitate a stonefly, while smaller sizes imitate caddis flies. They can be used successfully in places that have neither of those insects. It floats well and is easy to see on the water, so it's an excellent fly for beginners.

**Griffith's gnat:** It's designed to imitate a cluster of midges. It's bigger than the real thing, which makes it easier to fish. Midges hatch almost year-round and are found on most rivers.

**Joe's hopper:** Another hall of famer. It's a go-to summer pattern on rivers and many lakes. Fish it aggressively. Plop it on the water and twitch it a little and you can get some amazing strikes.

**Elk hair caddis:** Although it's a caddis imitation, it also mimics a stonefly and a hopper. It floats high in the water and is durable.

## NYMPH FISHING

This is effective when there are no insects hatching and fish are feeding below the surface. Anglers use imitations of aquatic insects to entice fish, typically by drifting a fly under water below an "indicator," which is a fly fishing term for a bobber. If you don't see fish rising, a nymph is often the best tactic.

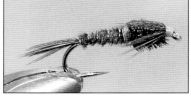
Pheasant tail

Like dry flies, they're naturally drifted with the current. The best fishing is usually in water less than 10 feet deep that is flowing at about walking pace. If the water is deep or swift, use split shot or similar weights to get the flies to sink quicker.

Nymphs are similar to traditional "wet flies," but wet flies imitate an insect that is about to get its wings.

### Fill your fly box with ...

**Hare's ear:** This is an excellent all-around pattern that resembles a caddis and other aquatic insects. Its mottled gray color is a fish magnet.

**Prince nymph:** This has a peacock herl for a body, and there is something about peacock feathers that fish love.

**Pheasant tail:** Pheasant tail fibers are sort of like peacock herls in their ability to attract fish. A pheasant tail imitates a lot of different mayfly larvae.

**Copper John:** This weird pattern looks like a robot fly, but it works. It sinks fast, which probably accounts for some of its effectiveness.

**Kauffman stonefly:** This is one of the most realistic-looking nymph patterns. It mimics an important trout food. It's large and heavy, which makes it a good lead fly in a tandem setup because it quickly sinks.

Rabbit leech

### STREAMER FISHING

Streamers imitate a living thing, like small fish, leeches or crawdads. Some don't imitate anything, but still attract fish. Streamers are similar to lures because they are cast and pulled, or stripped, back.

While many flies are allowed to naturally drift with the current, streamers are fished with lots of motion so they imitate a wounded fish or prey fleeing a predator.

### Fill your fly box with ...

**Woolly bugger:** There are more variations to this fly than any other, and probably few fish in the freshwater world that have not been caught by one. They come in a variety of colors, but black, brown and olive consistently work well.

**Clouser minnow:** Probably the most versatile fly in the world. It works well in fresh and saltwater.

**Leech:** Leeches are common in lakes, reservoirs and ponds, and imitations of them will catch multiple species of fish.

**Muddler minnow:** This imitates a variety of small prey fish that attract larger fish. Muddlers are tied with deer hair, which is buoyant, so you may need some weight or a sinking line to get them down to the fish.

# River tactics

Whether it's a big, broad river or a small backcountry creek, all streams share certain characteristics and harbor fish in predictable areas. Since most stream fishing is done for trout, steelhead and salmon, we will concentrate on those.

A river is like a treadmill. If fish are on it, they have to burn energy to stay in one spot. If they can find a break in the current, they get the advantage of the current bringing them food without having to fight its constant force.

This means fish rarely are evenly distributed throughout a river. They are concentrated in places where they can rest, feed or hide from predators. Some spots offer all three. These places are gold mines for trout anglers.

Being able to identify those places before you make your first cast means you will catch more fish.

If you are new to river fishing, start with smaller rivers and creeks where there is less water to cover and easier access.

In these streams, you often can wade or cast to prime water and easily position yourself to effectively fish each spot. After you've learned where fish like to hang out in a small stream, apply it to larger rivers.

Here's a look at some of those prime areas, why trout like them, and how to fish them.

## BOULDER GARDENS

Clumps of large rocks provide classic pocket water, which is the slower water you can find behind boulders in the river. The riverbed is typically steep and the water is moving fast, which creates lots of eddies, pour-overs and other interruptions in the current.

Trout like to lurk in pocket water, then dart into the current and grab food as it flows past.

When you fish pocket water, you're trying to provoke a quick, impulsive strike. Cast your tackle above a rock and let the current carry it past the rock and be ready for a fish to strike. If it's a big rock, try landing a spinner right in the eddy, then give it a quick tug to get its blade spinning and expect a strike right as it hits the fast current.

If nothing happens after a few casts, try a different spot.

## SUBMERGED ROCKS

If the water is too deep or murky to see submerged rocks, you can tell they are there by swirls, boils or depressions on the surface.

This is where trout may rest and where big fish often like to hang out. Depending on the speed of the river, you will have to cast upstream and let your tackle sink to the level of the rocks or put on heavier tackle to get down there.

Trout may be resting among the rocks and not aggressively feeding, so methodically cover the area. If you're not occasionally hanging up on the rocks, you're probably not getting deep enough.

## UNDERCUT BANKS

These are often on the outside corners of river bends, or where rivers meander through meadows. Trout love them, especially big brown trout. Undercuts, where the bank hangs over the river, give trout security and current sweeps food right to them.

Undercuts are perfect places to dead-drift a fly that imitates a terrestrial insect, like a grasshopper, beetle or ant. Keep your fly drifting a few inches from the bank. Savvy old brown trout will try to grab your fly and then streak back into the cutbank and tangle your line in the roots.

You can cast a lure upstream and let the current drift it into the undercut, then let your line come taut and your lure swing back into the current. It's risky because undercuts typically have lots of snags, but they are gold mines.

## EDDIES AND SEAMS

These are perfect feeding and resting areas for fish. The eddy is the swirling water behind a rock, a point or anything else that protrudes from the bank. The seam is where the downstream current and the swirling eddy currents meet.

If the eddy is on your side of the river, quietly and cautiously approach and gently flip some lightly weighted bait, such as worms or salmon eggs, into it. A noisy approach or a big splash will spook the trout. From the opposite side, cast upstream and across current and let your bait drift right along the seam.

## RIFFLES

This is where swift, shallow water flows over a cobbled bottom and makes a rippled surface. Riffles may seem too shallow and too swift to hold trout, but looks can be deceiving. Trout can put their bellies on the bottom and hold there nearly effortlessly.

Cutthroat and rainbows especially love riffles. They snatch food as it drifts past, and they camouflage themselves amazingly well against the cobbled bottom.

But riffles offer little protection from predators, so trout are easily spooked. Be stealthy.

Cast your lure across the current and swing it downstream until it is hanging directly below you, then repeat. Swing your lure through the entire riffle. Riffles are excellent places to drift large, high-floating dry flies. Trout can't resist them.

## SUBMERGED LOGS

Logs not only break up the current, they provide microhabitat in the river. Decaying wood provides food for insects, which in turn feed trout.

Trout love to rest and feed behind logs, and they tuck themselves between the branches where they are most protected from predators.

It often takes a close cast to lure out a trout. Logs can be a test of your casting accuracy. Aim wrong and you just donated your tackle to the river.

Trout often will grab your lure and streak back under the log. So be prepared — you might end the battle without a trout or your tackle.

## DEEP HOLES

These are the most mysterious parts of the river. They can hold schools of fish or be totally barren.

Cast weighted bait into the depths of the pool and wait, just as if you were lake fishing. Deep holes usually aren't prime feeding areas, but if fish are resting there, you might entice them to strike. Try different lures and vary the speed of your retrieve. Don't toss the same lure over and over and retrieve it at the same speed. Mix things up.

## OTHER TIPS

➤ Aquatic insects are the major food source in most rivers and streams. You can find out what types of insects are common by turning over rocks in shallow water and observing what's there.

➤ Don't anchor your bait to the bottom. It's unnatural for bait to be waving in the current like a flag in the breeze. Fish prefer a natural, drifting presentation. Use just enough weight to get your bait near the bottom and let the current carry it to the fish.

➤ Always be on the lookout for rising or cruising fish. You can often spot fish in a river, and if you carefully observe them, they give you good clues about how to catch them.

➤ Keep moving. You're usually better off presenting your bait, lures or flies to lots of different places and looking for aggressive fish.

➤ Fishing pressure can have a big effect on a river. If you get away from places that other anglers can easily reach, you improve your chances of catching fish.

➤ Catch-and-release tactics can greatly improve fishing on rivers. Many have special regulations for that reason. Even if they don't, releasing your fish or limiting your harvest will pay dividends later for you and future fishermen.

# Lake tactics

Lakes and reservoirs have a reputation for unpredictability. You can fish for hours without a strike one day and the next day the lake seems to be boiling with fish. Half the battle of fishing a large lake or reservoir is narrowing down where you want to concentrate your efforts. The other challenge is hitting the water when fishing is most likely to be prime, whether it's a time of day or a time of year. Here is some advice for improving your timing.

## SEASONAL CHANGES

A lake's water temperature is uniform only twice a year. Those periods are known as spring and fall turnover. They are important because they often coincide with the two times fish are most active.

### Spring

This often is the best time of year to fish a lake or reservoir. Fish are cold-blooded and become more active as the water warms. They also are coming out of a period of semi-hibernation when winter food supplies were limited.

Longer days and warmer water spark prime growing conditions for the plankton that form the base of the food chain. Spring also coincides with most spawning seasons, and growing reproductive organs require a lot of the fishes' energy. That sparks a feeding frenzy. Fish also become more aggressive as they compete for mates or protect their eggs or nests.

Shallow water warms more quickly than deeper water, bringing fish closer to shore in their search for food.

All these factors mean fishermen tend to catch more in spring.

## Summer

As spring turns to summer, the water gets the warmest closest to the surface and stratifies. Water near the surface stays warm and floats on a layer of colder, more dense water. Even fish that are warm-water tolerant, such as largemouth bass, don't like intense sunlight and will hold in the heavy cover of deep water to avoid it.

This is when you will typically find the fish a little deeper and more active early and late in the day and they seek water that is a few degrees cooler and sunlight that is less intense.

## Fall

Fall brings cooler water and another burst of activity. Fish aggressively feed to pack on weight for winter, or in the case of brown trout and other fish, prepare for spawning season.

## HABITAT

A lake's placid surface may make it seem uniform, but the underwater terrain varies. Look for coves, points, cliffs and man-made structures like dams and docks

to figure out where fish likely are holding.

If you have a depth finder, look for abrupt transitions, such as submerged islands, shelf edges and trenches. You also should try to identify the makeup of the bottom's surface. For instance, smallmouth bass like a rocky bottom better than mud or sand.

Look for vegetation along the shore that provides cover and possible food sources, such as insects, that might fall into the water.

Different species prefer different parts of the lake, and you need different tactics to target them. Many species travel in schools. Where you find one, you're likely to find more.

Some areas in large lakes and reservoirs are consistently more productive. Don't be shy about asking at local tackle shops what areas have good fishing. Also, pay attention to the obvious. If you see a lot of boats or bank anglers concentrating on a certain area, you might want to join them (at a reasonable distance, of course).

## LAKE FISHING TIPS

➤ Invest in a depth finder. It will help you understand the contour of the bottom. It also shows where fish are, but doesn't guarantee they will bite. Equally important, it shows where there are no fish so you won't waste your time. Many also have thermometers that gauge the temperature at different depths.

➤ If you don't have a fish finder, troll. Trolling lets you cover a lot of water in a relatively short amount of time. You can locate fish like bass and crappie by slowly trolling. Once you hook a fish or get a strike, concentrate on that area.

➤ Frequently alter your speed and direction when you're trolling. If you hold the same speed and direction, fish are more likely to follow your bait without striking. A change often triggers a strike. Trolling in a lazy serpentine pattern will often get you more strikes than trolling in a straight line.

➤ As a general rule, shallow water has more fish than deep water.

➤ Fish usually are closer to the surface in mornings and evenings, which makes them easier to locate and catch.

➤ Where a river or stream enters or exits a lake are good places to find fish.

➤ In summer, look for places with cooler water. During spring and fall, look for places with warmer water.

➤ Be patient. Fish in lakes often are influenced by subtle changes that we can't detect, which means they will often go on or off the bite for no apparent reason.

➤ Learn your lake. If you fish a lake or reservoir enough times you will start to see patterns of when and where fishing is best. It will help you maximize your fishing success later.

➤ Don't over-harvest. There's no limit on many of the species of fish found in lakes and reservoirs. When fishing is hot, it's easy to catch more than you will later want to clean or eat. Use your boat's live well or a submerged fish basket. Keep the best fish and release the rest.

# Lakes and reservoirs

## ALTURAS LAKE

### Quick facts
**What's there?** Kokanee, stocked trout, protected bull trout

**Nearest town:** Stanley

**Services:** Boat launch and outhouses

**Camping:** Forest Service sites around the lake

**Special fishing rules:** You have to release bull trout.

**Getting there:** From Stanley, take Idaho 78 about 25 miles south to the turnoff to the lake.

Where in Idaho? See map page 3, **G-5**

### Alturas lake scouting report
Idaho Fish and Game stocks the 1,200-acre lake with hatchery trout. There are kokanee salmon in the lake, but your results may vary. Some years you get a lot of small fish and other years you can pick up a few larger fish.

Alturas Lake is one of the more popular summer hangouts and you'll definitely want to reserve a campsite (www.reserveamerica.com) before going or you will be relegated to an undeveloped spot down the road.

# ANDERSON RANCH RESERVOIR

## Quick facts

**What's there?** Rainbow trout, kokanee salmon, smallmouth bass, yellow perch, protected bull trout

**Nearest town:** Pine

**Services:** Boat launches, outhouses, restaurants and lodges

**Camping:** There are several U.S. Forest Service campgrounds around the reservoir, which get busy in the summer months. It's hard to find a camping area when the kokanee are biting.

**Special fishing rules:** A daily bag limit of 25 kokanee (50 in possession).

**Getting there:** From Mountain Home, go east on U.S. 20 to Anderson Ranch Dam Road for the south end or take Pine/Featherville Road to the north end. From Fairfield go west on U.S. 20 to Pine/Featherville Road.

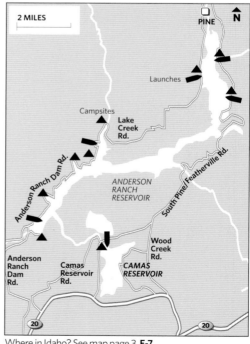

Where in Idaho? See map page 3, **E-7**

64

### Anderson Ranch Reservoir scouting report

It takes time to learn the ins and outs of this 4,740-acre reservoir, and some anglers make it their primary reservoir for fishing throughout the season. It's well known for its kokanee runs and can get hit hard during the peak season in July and August.

Kokanee run deep when the water warms up, so you'll want to follow them with downriggers and trolling gear like small Beer Cans or Ford Fenders. Anglers like to follow trolling gear with Wedding Ring spinners tipped with worms or another kind of bait.

Trout fishing can be good in the spring and fall when the fish are closer to the surface.

A fun way to fish the reservoir is to go after bass that can be lurking in the coves, especially in the summer.

## ARROWROCK RESERVOIR

### Quick facts

**What's there?** Rainbow trout, kokanee salmon, smallmouth bass, protected bull trout

**Nearest town:** Boise

**Services:** Boat launch and outhouse

**Camping:** All undeveloped sites

**Special fishing rules:** None

**Getting there:** From Boise, take Idaho 21 to the high bridge and go right on Middle Fork of the Boise River Road. Take it past Lucky Peak to Arrowrock.

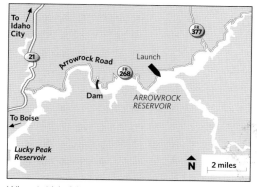

Where in Idaho? See map page 3, **D-6**

### Arrowrock reservoir scouting report

Don't take this 4,000-acre reservoir that's within minutes of Boise for granted. Fishing can be pretty good in the spring when trout are closer to the surface and cruising the shoreline looking for food.

In fact, bank fishing is popular in spring. Toss a marshmallow and a worm off shore and wait for the action.

The reservoir turns on again for trout in the fall as water temperatures cool and trout come closer to the bank.

Anglers do complain about pikeminnows in the summer because the unwanted fish come into the shallows and you can't get your bait past them to the trout.

The reservoir is popular with trollers, who use the same techniques as with other reservoirs. Troll with spinners or small crankbaits close to the surface in the spring and early summer and then try Wedding Ring spinners and bait in the summer when the water warms up and the trout dive deep.

Some anglers use boats to get to coves along the unroaded side of the reservoir to target bass.

Arrowrock Reservoir leaves a little to be desired for camping along the Middle Fork of the Boise River Road. However, some boaters prefer to boat camp on the opposite side of the reservoir, where they can have the coves all to themselves.

## BROWNLEE RESERVOIR

### Quick facts

**What's there?** Bass, crappie, bluegill, catfish, carp, perch, sturgeon, trout

**Nearest towns:** Cambridge and Pine Creek, Ore.

**Services:** Boat ramps, stores, restaurants, tackle and fuel at or near the reservoir

**Camping:** Woodhead Park and Steck Park are on the reservoir and there are lots of undeveloped sites. There are several campgrounds and undeveloped sites on the Oregon side.

**Special rules:** You can fish on the reservoir with a license from either Idaho or Oregon, but you can fish only from shore in the state for which you have a license.

**Getting there:** From Cambridge, take Idaho 71 east about 20 miles. You can access the upper end by going through Weiser and down to Steck Park.

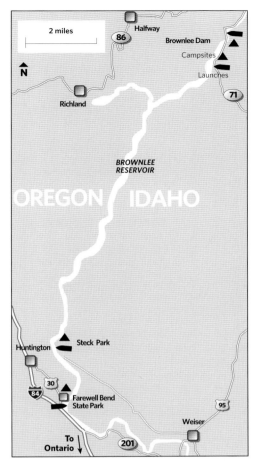

2 miles

N

Halfway

86

Brownlee Dam

Campsites

Launches

71

Richland

BROWNLEE
RESERVOIR

OREGON / IDAHO

Huntington

Steck Park

84

30

Farewell Bend
State Park

95

Weiser

To
Ontario

201

Where in Idaho? See map page 3, **A-3**

## Brownlee Reservoir scouting report

The 57-mile long, 15,000-acre reservoir is one of the best warmwater fisheries in the state. Anglers flock there for its spectacular crappie, bass and catfish populations, which have produced several state records.

Spring and early summer are the best times to fish at Brownlee. Thanks to Hells Canyon's mild weather, spring comes early, and fish start getting lively in March or April.

May is the best time, and if you can hit the water with a worm, you can probably catch a fish. Fishing remains good through the summer, but it can be blistering hot. You may have to search a little to find the schools when things cool off in the fall.

Bass is probably the most-targeted species at the reservoir, which hosts tournaments throughout the year. Bass can be taken on a variety of tackle, but crankbaits and plastics are the most common.

Use metallic crankbaits that rattle if you're fishing in murky water. Under normal conditions (at least a few feet of visibility) anything that resembles a crawdad works well for smallmouths.

Crappie will bite on bait or jigs. Bring lots of jigs in different colors. Fish will often favor one color over another and switch preferences.

The upper reservoir has a healthy population of catfish that usually are easy to catch in May and June. Steck Park northeast of Weiser is a good spot for them.

Because of Brownlee's size, boating is a popular way to fish, but there's reasonably good bank access along the roaded sections.

Boaters should be aware of the high winds that can suddenly rip through the canyon.

Despite its distance from major population areas, it's one of the most developed areas because of Idaho Power's series of dams — Brownlee, Oxbow and Hells Canyon — that provide a wealth of recreation facilities.

There are fully developed campgrounds with power, water and electricity, and undeveloped camping along the reservoirs. There are boat ramps and several places to buy fishing tackle and supplies.

## BRUNDAGE RESERVOIR

### Quick facts
**What's there?** Rainbow trout

**Nearest town:** McCall

**Services:** Unpaved boat launch and an outhouse

**Camping:** There are a few undeveloped spots along the shoreline.

**Special fishing rules:** Artificial flies and lures only. There is a two-fish limit (none less than 20 inches). Check the current Idaho Fish and Game rules book for details.

**Getting there:** From McCall, go northwest on Idaho 55 about 4 miles to the Goose Lake/Brundage Mountain turnoff. Take it past Brundage Mountain Resort, then go 2 miles and go right near the dam to the east side of the reservoir.

### Brundage Reservoir scouting report

This is a classic mountain lake that is relatively easy to reach, but expect some rough gravel roads. The reservoir is 270 acres and offers a rare combination of easy access and the chance for large trout in a mountain lake without hiking.

The reservoir has trophy rules, so you can keep only two fish and they must be longer than 20 inches, which for all practical purposes means it's catch and release since fish rarely grow that big there. But you will find a good trout population with fish in the low to mid teens in length.

This is a popular spot for float tubers and small boats, but motors are allowed. Nearly the entire east side of the reservoir is accessible by road and there's lots of bank access on that side. The west side is accessible only by boat or hiking.

This is a good place to troll spinners and cast and strip wet flies. You might find some bug hatches in the summer.

The reservoir is at 6,218 feet in elevation, so don't expect to get

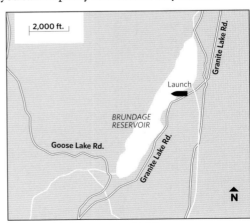

Where in Idaho? See map page 3, **C-2**

in there before Memorial Day. It fishes best in summer and fall. There are several other lakes within a short drive and lots of trails to other nearby lakes.

## BRUNEAU DUNES

### Quick facts
**What's there?** Largemouth bass, bluegill

**Nearest town:** Bruneau

**Services:** State park with a visitors center, toilets, picnic areas, boat launch

**Camping:** Sites at Bruneau Dunes State Park

**Special fishing rules:** There's a two-fish limit on bass (none less than 20 inches). No gas motors.

**Getting there:** From Mountain Home, go south on Idaho 51 and east on Idaho 78 to the park entrance.

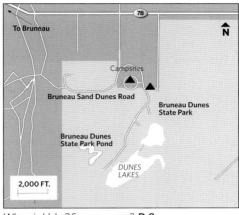

Where in Idaho? See map page 3, **D-8**

### Bruneau Dunes scouting report
Bruneau Dunes has two lakes totaling about 100 acres. It will cost you a $5 entrance fee per vehicle.

The restriction on largemouth bass essentially means it's catch and release because you're not likely to catch one that large. In good years you can catch lots of large bluegills, which are popular there, especially in May. There also are carp in the lake.

The lake has some classic bass water with much of the shore lined with reeds. There is some bank access as well. It's a good place for float tubes, pontoon boats and other small craft, but it can get windy.

The lake is at 2,500 feet in a mild climate, so it's a good spot for early spring fishing and offers year-round camping among the dunes.

# BULL TROUT LAKE

## Quick facts
**What's there?** Rainbow trout, brook trout

**Nearest town:** Stanley

**Services:** Outhouses

**Camping:** Forest Service campground

**Special fishing rules:** No motors allowed

**Getting there:** It's about midway between Lowman (34 miles) and Stanley (24 miles). Take Idaho 21 to Milepost 107 and turn west at the sign to Bull Trout Lake and go about 2 miles.

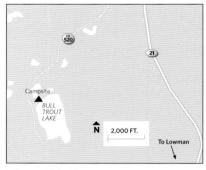

Where in Idaho? See map page 3, **E-4**

## Bull Trout Lake scouting report

This 90-acre lake is nestled in forested mountains, which makes it ideal and picturesque for camping and fishing.

You don't have to be an expert angler to catch the ever-so-feisty brook trout. Luckily, Idaho Fish and Game stocks the lake with rainbow trout in case you want something a little bigger. It's a great place to teach kids how to fish, especially because brookies can be eager to bite.

Although you can fish it from the bank, drifting or paddling around in a canoe or other small craft is the best and most pleasant way to fish.

The area has other developed and undeveloped camping areas close by and lots of hiking and motorcycling trails.

If you want to camp at Bull Trout Lake Campground you need to make reservations (www.reserveamerica.com) in advance. It is very popular in the summer.

## C.J. STRIKE RESERVOIR

### Quick facts
**What's there?** Bluegill, bullhead catfish, channel catfish, crappie, largemouth and smallmouth bass, rainbow trout, sturgeon, yellow perch, carp
**Nearest towns:** Bruneau and Grandview
**Services:** Boat launches. Black Sands resort is on the south side.
**Camping:** Several public and private campgrounds along the south shoreline.
**Special fishing rules:** None
**Getting there:** From Mountain Home, take Idaho 51 to the east side of the reservoir or take Grandview Road and C.J. Strike Dam Road to the west end.

### C.J. Strike Reservoir scouting report
This place almost deserves a guidebook of its own because it's so large and offers such diverse fishing. The reservoir is 7,500 acres, but it's formed by two rivers and several creeks, which give it different characteristics than your typical oval or oblong reservoir.

It's one of the most productive reservoirs in Idaho, but unlike other reservoirs it is almost always full of water. The dam is used for power generation, not flood control or to store irrigation water. You won't see the early-season high water or the late-season bathtub ring at C.J. Strike like you do at other large reservoirs.

Idaho Power and the Bureau of Land Management have upgraded their facilities in recent years, which means there's excellent camping, modern boat launches, docks and other amenities.

Like many reservoirs in Southwest Idaho, C.J. Strike is at its best in springtime. It has good-to-excellent fishing for bass, crappie, bluegill and catfish. In recent years, it's had some incredible crappie fishing.

Most of the bank access is near the dam or along the south side of the reservoir off Idaho 78 between Grandview and Bruneau. The head of the reservoir in the Snake River arm can be accessed at Loveridge Bridge on Idaho 51 south of Mountain Home.

Because of its size and diversity of habitat — from broad, shallow flats to deep holes with sheer bluffs that rise out of the reservoir — you have an amazing variety of places to fish. The lower end around the dam has several parks. The south shore around Black Sands Resort, Cove Recreation Area, Cottonwood Campground and Jack's Creek at the C.J. Strike Wildlife Management Area offer good bank access and fun places to fish.

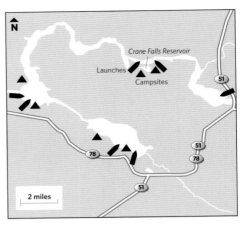

Where in Idaho? See map page 3, **D-8**

It's difficult to say what tackle works best because there are so many different types of fish that require different tactics. But the nice thing about the reservoir is there's almost always something biting. Bring an assortment of crappie jigs, plastics (rubber worms), a few crankbaits for bass, and some nightcrawlers. Odds are pretty good you will catch something.

Idaho Power has heavily stocked the reservoir with rainbow trout, which provide good fishing when the reservoir's water cools and the warmwater fishing slows.

If you're a boater, you pretty much have your run of the reservoir. There's a lot of water to cover and you will probably want to focus on specific areas, like the area around the dam, the Snake River or the Bruneau River arm. There are miles of undeveloped and difficult-to-access sections of the reservoir. There's also private shoreline, so make sure you know where you are if you decide to get off on land.

The reservoir can get very windy at times and anglers in small crafts should be cautious of rough water that could swamp or capsize a boat.

## CLEAR LAKE

### Quick facts
**What's there?** Rainbow trout
**Nearest town:** Buhl
**Services:** Clubhouse has a bar and restaurant
**Camping:** None
**Special fishing rules:** Catch and release only; $10 per day to fish (prices subject to change). For current prices and stocking information, call (208) 543-4849.
**Getting there:** Take Interstate 84 to Exit 157 near Wendell. Go south and then west

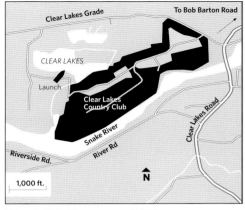

Where in Idaho? See map page 3, **H-9**

on Bob Barton Road and watch for the signs to Clear Lakes Country Club.

### Clear Lake scouting report

This private lake is popular for winter fly fishing. It's usually stocked in November and again around January or February.

The lake is usually fished with float tubes, pontoon boats and other small craft. It's spring fed and maintains a constant temperature of about 60 degrees so you can comfortably float tube. There is limited bank access, but some fishing is available to shore anglers. The lake typically has big trout in it, and sometimes real monsters in the 3- to 5-pound range.

Several years ago, the lake had some problems with fish disappearing, but that seems to have been solved. The fish come from nearby private hatcheries and are fun to catch, but will sometimes go off the bite and can be challenging to hook. Leeches, woolly buggers and similar lake patterns typically work well, as well as small nymphs like pheasant tails and Copper Johns.

When the weather warms, aquatic plants start to grow and make fishing difficult, so plan your trip for late fall or spring.

## CRANE FALLS RESERVOIR/COVE ARM

### Quick facts
**What's there?** Bass, bluegill, crappie, largemouth and smallmouth bass, trout
**Nearest town:** Bruneau
**Services:** Outhouse and boat launch
**Camping:** Unimproved sites around the reservoir
**Special fishing rules:** A limit of two bass a day (none less than 20 inches). Motorboats are not allowed on Crane Falls. Check the current Fish and Game rules book.

**Getting there:** From Mountain Home, go south on Idaho 51, cross the Snake River and look for Crane Falls Road on the right. Follow the road to the reservoir and Cove Arm.

### Crane Falls Reservoir scouting report

Crane Falls (84 acres) and Cove Arm (76 acres) are fun places to fish and great for a float tube, cataraft, canoe or kayak. They have healthy populations of bass and bluegill and some trout. You have a chance to land a trophy-size largemouth bass.

Crane Falls can have excellent bluegill fishing in the spring, and it's a great time to take kids for nearly non-stop action. Crappie will take almost anything you put in the water — bait, small jigs or flies.

Cove Arm is just beyond Crane Falls and is a lagoon-like reservoir that

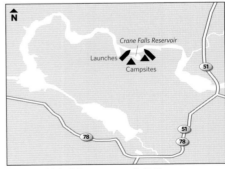

Where in Idaho? See map page 3, **D-8**

is attached to the Snake River through a small opening in a dike. Anglers can fish either side of the dike for bass and crappie. It provides a unique bass fishing opportunity. Inside the dike, you're likely to catch largemouth bass. On the river side, you're more likely to catch smallmouths and crappie.

As summer progresses, weeds grow in these waters, which makes fishing more challenging, especially from shore.

There are still plenty of opportunities to fish along the edges of the weed beds from a boat or float tube. Anglers can catch bluegill and bass by getting down near the bottom with plastic worms.

Have tackle to target any of the species you're likely to encounter. A small collection of jigs, plastic worms, crankbaits and some bait should cover things. If you're a fly angler, bigger is typically better for bass. Cast streamers like bunny leeches, Clouser minnows or marabou leeches.

If bass are rising in the evenings, deer-hair poppers or foam poppers can get you some exciting fishing. During summer, have some weedless hooks to keep a fly from snagging on the grass.

## DEADWOOD RESERVOIR

### Quick facts
**What's there?** Kokanee salmon, trout

**Nearest town:** Garden Valley

**Services:** Boat ramps, airstrip

**Camping:** Several developed and undeveloped sites around the reservoir

**Special fishing rules:** Limit of 25 kokanee per day and 50 in possession.

**Getting there:** From Garden Valley, take the Banks-to-Lowman Highway about a half mile past Milepost 23. Go north on the Scott Mountain Road (Forest Service Road 555) for about 24 miles to the reservoir. It's a long, steep, rough road. An alternative route for people

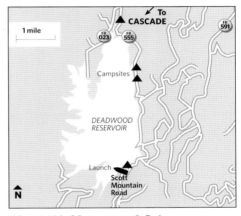

Where in Idaho? See map page 3, **D-4**

with RVs or boat trailers is the north end of the reservoir through Cascade and the Warm Lake Highway.

### Deadwood Reservoir scouting report

This isolated mountain reservoir at 5,300 feet can be a challenge to get to. You have to cross higher mountains to reach it, so it's often inaccessible until June and sometimes as late as July.

The quality of fishing varies from year to year, but there's a good kokanee population and trout fishing can range from fair to good. Spring and late summer usually have good trolling for kokanee. Also, you can try bait fishing for trout near the dam.

In recent years the reservoir has produced some huge rainbow trout. It can be difficult to catch them because they are rare, but a few 8- to 10-pounders come out

of the reservoir every year.

If you're planning to troll for kokanee, be prepared to go deep with downriggers or heavy trolling gear. A fish finder is a valuable tool for locating schools.

Deadwood is 3,000 acres with 21 miles of shoreline and good access for bank anglers on the east side and north end.

There is ample shoreside camping on the east side, which is developed, and the west side is pristine forest. There are several boat ramps, but be careful hauling a boat over the rough, steep road.

The reservoir usually starts full in the spring and is drained throughout the summer. Despite its remoteness you can expect plenty of people looking for someplace to escape the heat during the peak summer months.

## GOOSE LAKE

### Quick facts

**What's there?** Rainbow trout, brook trout

**Nearest town:** McCall

**Services:** Boat launch, outhouses

**Camping:** There's a Forest Service campground on the south end and undeveloped camping on north end.

**Special fishing rules:** None

**Getting there:** From McCall, take Idaho 55 northwest 4 miles to the Brundage/Goose Lake Road. Turn right and travel 9 miles to the lake.

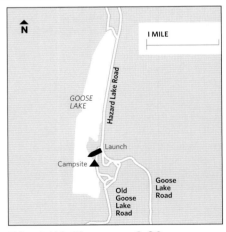

Where in Idaho? See map page 3, **C-2**

### Goose Lake scouting report

This high-elevation (6,400 feet) lake is a great summer get-away, but don't

plan on getting there any earlier. It usually isn't clear of snow until mid June and sometimes not until July. It's 520 acres, which is pretty large for a mountain lake, but not too big for float tubes and small craft. There's a boat launch near Grouse Campground for larger craft.

The lake has stocked rainbow trout and brook trout. It has a pretty short growing season, so fish don't get very large. The brook trout are self-sustaining, and Fish and Game allows a generous 25-fish limit on them. Most will probably run in the 6- to 8-inch range.

Because of the short growing season, fish in mountain lakes tend to be aggressive. You can catch them by bank fishing with bait or trolling spinners or trolling gear.

There are numerous other backcountry lakes nearby. The Hazard Lakes are right up the road and you can hike to several other lakes.

## HORSETHIEF RESERVOIR

### Quick facts
**What's there?** Rainbow and brown trout
**Nearest town:** Cascade
**Services:** Boat launches
**Camping:** Lots of free sites on the south end
**Special fishing rules:** None
**Getting there:** From Cascade, take Warm Lake Highway about 6 miles to the Horsethief Reservoir turnoff on the right. Follow it about 3 miles to the reservoir.

### Horsethief Reservoir scouting report
This is a great place for fishing and camping. It's a short drive from Cascade in a picturesque mountain setting. There's lots of public camping near the water, as well as public fishing docks and ramps for small boats.

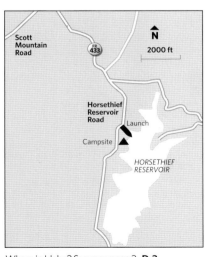

Where in Idaho? See map page 3, **D-3**

77

The reservoir is 1,270 acres and equally popular with fly anglers, bait dunkers and trollers. It's the perfect size for float tubes, canoes and other small boats.

You can catch a lot of fish from the bank with PowerBait or a worm and marshmallow, which makes it a good place to take beginners and kids.

The Idaho Department of Fish and Game drained and poisoned Horsethief in 2006 to get rid of unwanted perch, which tend to take over small bodies of water. The agency restocked it with rainbow and brown trout, which have flourished.

Because Fish and Game owns the reservoir and controls the water supply, it stays full year-round. The agency regularly stocks it with catchable and fingerling trout.

Fishing is consistently good, but don't expect any trophies. Because of its popularity and easy access, expect crowds, especially during peak summer and holiday weekends. October and early November are great times to go if you want good fishing and fewer people.

Horsethief is a popular ice fishing spot, too, but check road conditions before you go. Some years the road is plowed all the way to the reservoir. There's usually a plowed parking area.

## LAKE BILLY SHAW

**Quick facts**
   **What's there?** Trophy rainbow trout
   **Nearest town:** Owyhee, Nev.
   **Services:** Boat launches
   **Camping:** Fee sites
   **Special fishing rules:** $25 daily fishing fee. Fly fishing only. Harvest limited to one rainbow trout between 16 and 19 inches. Check www.shopaitribes.org for rule changes. The season is April 1 through October 31.
   **Getting there:** From Mountain Home, take

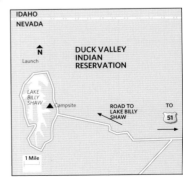

Where in Nevada? See map page 3, **D-9**

78

Idaho 51 south to the Duck Valley Indian Reservation. Look on the right for large signs that lead to the reservoir.

### Lake Billy Shaw scouting report

This has become a popular trophy lake for fly anglers because large, hard-fighting rainbow trout are common. This mid-sized (430 acres) reservoir is popular with float tubers and other small craft. Electric motors are allowed, but not gas engines.

The reservoir is in the high desert at about 5,300 feet. It is fertile and grows fish fast. The tribe typically stocks it in the fall and spring.

Trout in the 14- to 18-inch range are common and occasionally fish exceed 20 inches, but few get much larger than that. But what these trout lack in length, they make up for in strength. They are stout, broad fish that usually put up a fight greater than their actual size.

Spring is the prime fishing time, especially during May, when the reservoir gets the most anglers. Good fishing typically continues until late June or July, when moss beds form and make fishing more difficult. Fishing resumes in the fall when the moss beds break down and fish start aggressively feeding.

Lake Billy Shaw's rainbows tend to be fairly easy to catch during prime times. Anglers use standard stillwater patterns such as leeches and woolly buggers in dark colors. Casting and stripping nymphs like Copper Johns, Prince nymphs and damsel nymphs works well. Some anglers will run a leech trailed by a nymph. Anglers can get dry-fly action with damsels or midges, especially on calm afternoons and evenings.

Billy Shaw tends to get windy in the afternoon, and gusts can be strong enough to clear everyone off the reservoir. Get there early if you want to get a full day of fishing.

# LAKE CASCADE

## Quick facts
**What's there?** Rainbow trout, coho salmon, smallmouth bass, crappie, perch, kokanee, catfish, tiger muskie

**Nearest town:** Cascade

**Services:** State parks, boat ramps, day-use areas, motels and restaurants in Cascade

**Camping:** There are 16 sites around the lake run by Idaho Parks and Recreation or the U.S. Forest Service.

**Special fishing rules:** None

**Getting there:** The reservoir is west of Cascade, and roads run parallel to most of the shoreline with numerous access points.

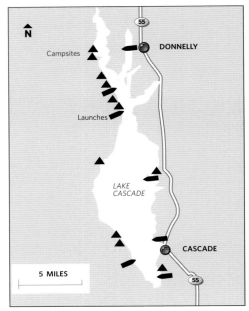

Where in Idaho? See map page 3, **C-3**

## Lake Cascade scouting report
At 28,300 acres, it is one of the largest reservoirs in the state and at one time was the most popular fishing spot in the state. It has a good variety of fish and excellent access. The nearby city of Cascade makes it convenient.

The lake is primarily known for its trout and smallmouth bass. The perch population crashed years ago, and Fish and Game has been working diligently to restore

them by killing predatory northern pikeminnow and stocking thousands of adult perch. Fish and Game's goal is to get a self-perpetuating perch population, but it may take a few years.

Trollers can often take limits of trout that average a couple pounds each. Fish can be taken on large trolling rigs trailed by Wedding Ring spinners and bait.

During the summer, trolling is the best bet. The lake is relatively shallow, so you don't need downriggers to get to the fish. Serious trollers may want to spool some leadcore trolling line, which helps them get to where the fish are.

One of the best times of the year for bank anglers is right after the ice thaws. Find a sandy beach and toss out a worm and a marshmallow.

The reservoir has a small population of tiger muskies. If you catch one, it must be at least 40 inches long before you can keep it.

Lake Cascade is a popular spot for ice fishing, which usually starts mid December or January. Parks and Recreation keeps several parking lots cleared on the east side of the lake near the golf course for easy access to the ice.

## LAKE LOWELL

### Quick facts
**What's there?** Largemouth and smallmouth bass, bluegill, crappie, catfish
**Nearest towns:** Nampa and Caldwell
**Services:** There are several paved boat ramps on the north side to launch boats, and more access points on the south side where you can launch a small boat, canoe, kayak or float tube.
**Camping:** None
**Special fishing rules:** There are limits on when and what size of bass you can keep. Motorized boats are allowed only from April 15 to Oct. 1. Check the current Fish and Game rules book.
**Getting there:** Head south from Nampa or Caldwell. There are numerous access points.

Where in Idaho? See map page 3, **B-6**

## Lake Lowell scouting report

Lake Lowell is a bit of an enigma. At 10,000 acres, it's one of the largest reservoirs in Southwest Idaho and has numerous species of game fish, but it gets considerably less pressure than other reservoirs like C.J. Strike and Brownlee. That is odd considering how close it is Idaho's population center.

There are several factors that may contribute to that. It has 28 miles of shoreline, but much of it is difficult to get to. Boats are the preferred method for many anglers. The lake is shallow and gets very weedy in the summer, which makes fishing difficult. Water levels also fluctuate throughout the year.

Abundant and trophy-sized largemouth bass probably are the lake's biggest draw. If you want to catch largemouths, this probably is as good a place as you will find in Southwest Idaho. Spring is a great time to fish because the shallow lake warms quickly when sunny weather arrives and the bass move into the shorelines to spawn. Savvy anglers can catch bass in thick weed beds during summer as well, but it's tough to get them out of the brush.

Other species aren't as plentiful or they're harder to catch than at other reservoirs, so it doesn't attract hordes of casual anglers. Despite that, there are often reports of large crappie, bluegill and catfish caught from the lake. The "hot bite" never seems to last long, but the fish are out there.

## LITTLE CAMAS RESERVOIR

### Quick facts

**What's there?** Rainbow trout
**Nearest town:** Mountain Home
**Services:** Boat launch and outhouse
**Camping:** The privately owned Fort Running Bear campground is near the reservoir. There's unimproved camping along the reservoir.
**Special fishing rules:** None
**Getting there:** From Mountain Home, take U.S. 20 about 26 miles to the reservoir.

### Little Camas Reservoir scouting report

Drought and thirsty irrigators have been hard on this 1,450-acre reservoir, but when it has water, it has good trout fishing. If it holds water for back-to-back years, it also has big trout. In the past few years that hasn't happened, so the

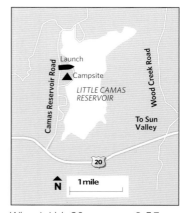

Where in Idaho? See map page 3, **E-7**

reservoir has been a spring fishery for stocked rainbow trout. By summer, it's too low and warm for most trout to survive. Fish and Game has suspended limit restrictions several times in the last five years to allow anglers to catch fish that would otherwise die.

Despite its tough times, it still has decent trout fishing in the spring. It has good bank access and it's the right size for float tubes or trolling. Since you will be catching planted trout, worms and marshmallows work well. You can troll with spinners or trolling rigs. Fly anglers will catch fish with common stillwater patterns like woolly buggers and leeches.

## LITTLE PAYETTE LAKE

### Quick facts
**What's there?** Rainbow trout, smallmouth bass, tiger muskie

**Nearest town:** McCall

**Services:** Boat launch, outhouse

**Camping:** A few undeveloped spots. Ponderosa State Park is a few miles away

**Special fishing rules:** A limit of two bass a day (none less than 20 inches). Check the current Fish and Game rules booklet for more details.

**Getting there:** From Idaho 55 in downtown McCall, take East Park Street to Davis Street and follow it

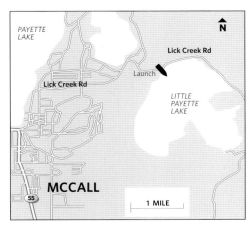

Where in Idaho? See map page 3, **C-2**

to Lick Creek Road, which will take you to the lake.

### Little Payette Lake scouting report

This 1,450-acre lake is at the upper elevations for smallmouth bass, but still produces some nice fish, typically in the spring when they come into the shore to spawn. The reservoir has lots of dead timber standing and log jams near shore. Bass like those areas and anglers like to lure them out.

The lake is stocked with rainbow trout, which can provide good angling. It's a tricky lake and the fish are very difficult to pattern. You can catch them by trolling or fly fishing from a float tube, but it's hard to catch them in good quantities. The lake has an overabundance of trash fish, which hurts its ability to grow trout like it once did.

If you're not having much luck fishing here, consider some of the nearby mountain lakes. There's Scout Pond near the head of the lake, which is a small pond stocked with catchable rainbow trout. There are trailheads to several mountain lakes farther up Lick Creek Road that typically offer good fishing during the summer.

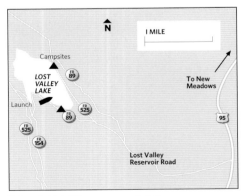

Where in Idaho? See map page 3, **B-2**

## LOST VALLEY RESERVOIR

### Quick facts
**What's there?** Rainbow trout
**Nearest town:** New Meadows
**Services:** Boat launches, outhouses

**Camping:** Two developed Forest Service campgrounds and lots of unimproved camping near the reservoir

**Special fishing rules:** None
**Getting there:** From New Meadows, go 8 miles south on U.S. 95. From Council go 16 miles north, then turn west on Lost Valley Reservoir Road (Forest Service road 089) near Pine Ridge. The reservoir is about 4 miles up the road.

### Lost Valley scouting report

This mid-elevation mountain reservoir is easy to get to and has good fishing in the summer. It's 1,630 acres and at 4,766 feet in a snow zone, so it usually isn't accessible until late spring. Even then it's likely to be cold. But it's a good escape from the summer heat and a fun place to fish for trout. The reservoir is stocked with rainbows and has a good carryover of fish from year to year, so fish in the mid teens are common.

This is an irrigation reservoir, so it gets drained down by the end of summer. It'll still be fishable, but not as scenic, and you may have to go through mud or sand to get to the shoreline.

Bait fishing or trolling lures is a good bet here. Fly anglers can use a float tube and standard lake patterns. There's good bank access and bait fishing from shore is a good option.

You can find trout in the stream sections above and below the reservoir, but the streams are not open year-round. You may find small brook trout very plentiful in the stream above the reservoir.

## LUCKY PEAK RESERVOIR

### Quick facts
**What's there?** Rainbow trout, smallmouth bass, kokanee salmon
**Nearest town:** Boise
**Services:** Boat launches, marina with fuel and a store, parks
**Camping:** None
**Special fishing rules:** None
**Getting there:** Take Idaho 21 from Boise to the reservoir

### Lucky Peak Reservoir scouting report

The 2,850-acre lake is more friendly to boat anglers in the spring and fall when there isn't the hustle and bustle of summer pleasure boaters.

Anglers who know the lake and follow the water temperatures know fishing can

be good in the colder months when trout will be closer to the surface and cruising the shoreline for food.

In mid-summer, if you want to compete with water skiers, you can go a little deeper with your trolling gear to hook into nice-size trout.

The lake gets a good share of fingerling trout, which can grow to from 12 to 14 inches.

Early in the spring, sometimes all it takes is a spinner running just beneath the surface to hook into trout. Perch-colored Rapalas are popular trolling lures for trout.

Lucky Peak's kokanee salmon have been getting more interest from anglers in recent years. They tend to run deep, so you need downriggers or leadcore line. An electronic fish finder can be a big help in locating schools.

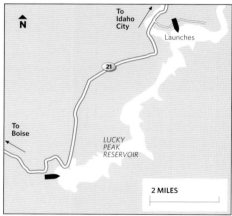

Where in Idaho? See map page 3, **C-6**

## MAGIC RESERVOIR

### Quick facts

**What's there?** Rainbow trout, brown trout, perch, smallmouth bass
**Nearest town:** Fairfield

**Services:** Boat launches, outhouses, a bar/restaurant/tackle shop on the west side.

**Camping:** There is a campground on the lake, but there are a lot of homes nearby.

**Special fishing rules:** There are special boundaries for where you can fish. Check the current Idaho Fish and Game rules book for specifics.

**Getting there:** From Fairfield, travel east to West Magic Road. This road is sometimes closed in winter. From the Shoshone area, go north on Idaho 75 to West Magic Road or East Magic Road.

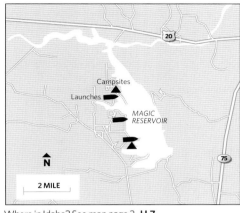

Where in Idaho? See map page 3, **H-7**

## Magic Reservoir scouting report

This 3,700-acre reservoir is a great place to catch perch. Trollers take rainbow and brown trout in the deep water, and bank anglers get them from shore.

Magic is a popular spot for fly anglers, who ply the shallow areas near the dam. The reservoir has one of the healthiest perch populations in the state that provides year-round fishing.

Magic's fishing tends to run hot and cold. It can provide excellent fishing at times for large trout, and people can catch them from shore or from boats or float tubes. Your best chance at trout is typically late spring in May or June. During

high-water years the shallow water at the head of the reservoir can provide excellent fly fishing. Summer can provide good fishing, but it can have long dead periods when fish either go deep or completely off the bite.

The reservoir's not a great fishery for bass because it's at 4,944 feet and has a fairly short growing season, but you can still catch them there.

All fish feed on perch (even perch), and any lure or fly that mimics a perch is likely to catch some fish. Gold-colored Rapalas will catch trout, and the Stayner ducktail is a popular fly that was originally tied to imitate the reservoir's young perch. Magic is one of the most popular places in the state for ice fishing, which usually starts in late December or January and lasts through February.

## MANN CREEK RESERVOIR

### Quick facts
**What's there?** Rainbow trout, smallmouth bass, crappie

**Nearest town:** Weiser

**Services:** Boat launches and outhouses. The Mann Creek Store is about 3 miles away on U.S. 95.

**Camping:** There's a nicely developed Forest Service campground on the northwest end.

**Special fishing rules:** None

**Getting there:** From Weiser, go 15 miles north on U.S. 95 and take Upper Mann Creek Road to the reservoir.

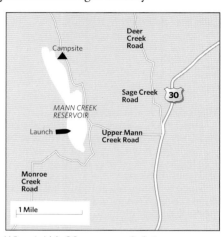

Where in Idaho? See map page 3, **A-4**

### Mann Creek Reservoir scouting report
This 280-acre irrigation reservoir sits at about 2,800 feet in elevation in

rolling hills and sagebrush country. It's been off the fishing radar for a lot of anglers except the locals. Folks often bypass it on their way to more popular places like Brownlee Reservoir. But anglers who fish there are discovering it can produce good trout and smallmouth bass. You may find some crappie as well, but if that's your game you may want to continue on to Brownlee.

Mann Creek Reservoir receives generous stockings of rainbow trout and has some wild fish. Fish and Game typically stocks fish in the spring and fall because summer temperatures get too high for the fish to thrive. However, the reservoir is deep enough to keep cold water and carry over the surviving fish to the next year. Like most Southwest Idaho reservoirs, spring and early summer are prime fishing times. Try trolling with spinners or trolling rigs for trout. Fish the dam with crankbaits for smallmouth. You can catch trout with bait from shore.

Bass can withstand warmer water, so if that's what you're after, you can probably catch them throughout the summer. This reservoir is worth fishing in the fall, too. You're probably going to encounter the ring of sandy, muddy or rocky shoreline as the water recedes. Launching a boat could be more challenging, but trout will become active after the summer heat passes and the water cools. Use the same tactics you used in spring.

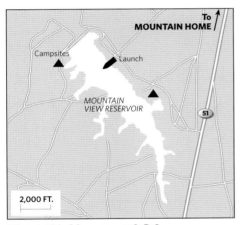

Where in Idaho? See map page 3, **D-9**

## MOUNTAIN VIEW RESERVOIR

### Quick facts
**What's there?** Rainbow trout
**Nearest town:** Owyhee, Nev.
**Services:** Stores, fuel and tribal licenses in Owyhee; boat launches at the lake
**Camping:** Fee camping at the lake
**Special fishing rules:** A tribal license is required for $10 per day for adults and $7.50 for youth 12 years and younger. The limit is five fish per day for adults and four for youth. No live bait is allowed except earthworms. Open year-round.
**Getting there:** From Mountain Home, take Idaho 51 south to the Duck Valley Indian Reservation. Look on the right for large signs leading to the reservoir.

### Mountain View Reservoir scouting report
At 633 acres, Mountain View is larger than Billy Shaw, closer to the highway and managed as a stocked fishery. That means fish are typically smaller than those in Lake Billy Shaw, but Mountain View tends to produce a few fish that top the largest ones in Billy Shaw. Mountain View has produced trout up to 8 pounds.

Mountain View is a good size and shape for trolling in a larger boat and fishing the many coves in a smaller craft or float tube. Gas motors are allowed. There are lots of bank fishing spots along the reservoir and a road along the dam where anglers have easy access to the reservoir and their vehicles if they prefer leisurely shoreline fishing.

Many people are content with fishing a worm and marshmallow off the bottom or suspended beneath a bobber and they catch plenty of fish that way. Others like trolling with either large trolling rigs in the main reservoir or smaller tackle in the coves. Although Billy Shaw is often favored by fly anglers for its bigger fish, they also do well at Mountain View casting and stripping flies similar to those used at Billy Shaw. While the fish are smaller, typically ranging from 10 to 15 inches, they are still hard fighters that will aggressively take flies.

The reservation makes a great weekend trip, and anglers will often fish Billy Shaw one day and Mountain View the next. There's nice camping along the reservoirs and excellent scenery with mountains looming in the background.

Like Billy Shaw, Mountain View is prone to strong afternoon winds, especially in the spring. It also gets big moss beds during the summer, which break down in the fall.

## OSTER LAKES

### Quick facts
**What's there?** Mostly rainbow trout
**Nearest town:** Hagerman
**Services:** Stores, gas, motels and restaurants in Hagerman
**Camping:** None on-site, but there are campgrounds nearby
**Special fishing rules:** Special seasons apply to waters at The Hagerman Wildlife Management Area. Check current rules.
**Getting there:** From Hagerman, go south on U.S. 30 and look for signs to the Hagerman Wildlife Management Area and state fish hatchery.

## Oster Lakes scouting report

This is a great place to take young or inexperienced anglers who want to catch trout. It's also a fun place for experienced anglers who want to catch lots of fish.

The lakes are next to the Hagerman hatchery, where Idaho Fish and Game raises millions of trout each year. Those fish are generously stocked in the lakes and provide a lot of action. Since the fish are straight out of the hatchery, they are usually gullible.

Fish and Game sometimes stocks surprises in the ponds — like sturgeon, bass or bluegill — to give anglers something else to catch.

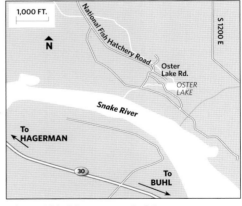

Where in Idaho? See map page 3, **G-9**

If fishing is slow there are lots of other things to do. You can tour the hatchery, feed fish in the raceways, and watch fish in the viewing ponds.

The ponds are home to birds and other wildlife, and Hagerman is the heart of the Thousand Springs scenic area, where you can find several other spring-fed lakes and ponds and the Malad River and Billingsley Creek.

## OXBOW/HELLS CANYON RESERVOIRS

### Quick facts
**What's there?** Bass, crappie, perch, bluegill, catfish, trout, carp, sturgeon

**Nearest town:** Pine Creek, Ore.

**Services:** Boat launches and a small store at the head of Oxbow Reservoir

**Camping:** Several developed campgrounds and lots of undeveloped camping areas along the reservoirs

**Special fishing rules:** There are limits on when and what size of bass you can keep. Check the current Fish and Game rules book.

**Getting there:** From Cambridge take Idaho 71, which crosses into Oregon below Brownlee Dam and then back into Idaho after Oxbow Dam.

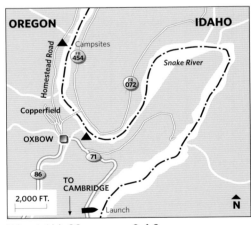

Where in Idaho? See map page 3, **A-2**

### Oxbow/Hells Canyon scouting report
Hells Canyon Reservoir is 2,500 acres and Oxbow is about 1,500. Both are long and narrow, much smaller than Brownlee, and more friendly for smaller boats.

Part of the fun of fishing the reservoirs is you never know what you will catch. There are dozens of different lures and baits that will work, but here's a hint: A small crappie jig, swirly tail rubber worm (like a Mister Twister) with a lead head or a small crankbait will catch almost everything. Big lures will exclude many of the smaller fish, such as crappie and bluegill, which can add a lot of action to your fishing.

Both reservoirs split Idaho and Oregon. Anglers can fish either reservoir with a valid fishing license from either state. They can launch and land a boat from either shore to fish, but anglers cannot fish from the shore on the Oregon side with an Idaho license, and vice versa.

The reservoirs are easily accessible by boat and from shore. The best bank access is on the Oregon side, so you will need an Oregon fishing license.

There are numerous boat ramps. Watch the weather if you plan to use a small craft. The canyon can get very windy, which causes choppy water. There is current in both reservoirs, so if you are rowing or paddling, take that into consideration. If you row with the current, it's going to take a lot more effort to get back.

One of the advantages of Oxbow and Hells Canyon reservoirs is that they are rarely drawn down, so all the boat ramps and waterfront campsites are available year-round.

The area offers excellent camping, especially in early spring. There's abundant wildlife and nearby hiking trails. The reservoirs fish well throughout the summer, but be prepared for intense heat. The good fishing continues into fall and many anglers try their luck for steelhead below Hells Canyon Dam.

## PADDOCK RESERVOIR

### Quick facts
**What's there?** Bass, bluegill, crappie, catfish, trout
**Nearest town:** Payette
**Services:** Unpaved boat launch
**Camping:** Some undeveloped camping
**Special fishing rules:** None
**Getting there:** Take Idaho 52 east from Payette and north on Little Willow Road to Paddock Valley Road.

### Paddock Reservoir scouting report
This reservoir is listed at 1,300 acres, but that's probably optimistic. It's a large, shallow irrigation reservoir that supplies a lot of thirsty farmers and ranchers. In good water years, which have been

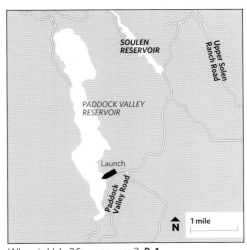

Where in Idaho? See map page 3, **B-4**

in short supply lately, it can produce excellent crappie, bluegill and bass fishing. During dry years it often gets drained to minimum pool, which is a fraction of its size when full, and the fish populations suffer.

The reservoir will almost always produce some decent bass fishing, but it seems

to take several years of back-to-back good water years for its crappie and bluegill to thrive. You might catch a catfish incidental to other fishing. Fish and Game sometimes stocks trout in the spring, but if that's what you're after you probably should go elsewhere. Spring or early summer is the best time to fish it.

Expect to drive over some very bumpy dirt and gravel roads, which can be tough on boats and trailers, to get there.

## SAGEHEN RESERVOIR

### Quick facts
**What's there?** Rainbow trout
**Nearest towns:** Smiths Ferry and Ola
**Services:** Boat launches
**Camping:** Several Forest Service campgrounds
**Special fishing rules:** None
**Getting there:** From Horseshoe Bend or Emmett, take Idaho 52 then turn north on Ola Road. Go north of Ola until it turns to gravel and take Forest Service roads 618 and 626 about 18 miles to the reservoir. From Smiths Ferry, take Forest Service roads 644 and 626 west to Sagehen.

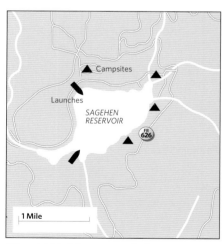

Where in Idaho? See map page 3, **C-4**

### Sagehen Reservoir scouting report
This 180-acre reservoir in the timber

---

94

at about 4,800 feet is a cool place to escape the summer heat. The fishing is pretty straightforward. Fish and Game stocks rainbow trout in reasonable quantities, typically starting in late spring when the snow melts and the lake is accessible. You can catch trout from shore or by trolling spinners from a boat. Don't expect big catch rates or big fish. You might get an occasional fish that survives a couple of seasons, but you're more likely to catch 10- to 12-inchers. The reservoir gets a lot of pressure because it's a popular camping area, but you can have some good fishing days. The reservoir is a good size for canoes, float tubes and other small craft.

## STANLEY LAKE

### Quick facts
**What's there?** Rainbow trout, kokanee salmon, lake trout

**Nearest town:** Stanley

**Services:** Boat launch, outhouses

**Camping:** Several Forest Service campgrounds near the lake and unimproved camping nearby

**Special fishing rules:** None

**Getting there:** From Stanley, go 4½ miles west of Stanley on Idaho 21. Turn on Stanley Lake Road and drive 3 miles on Forest Service road 455.

### Stanley Lake scouting report
Touring kayakers and canoeists love this 130-acre lake in the shadow of the peaks of the Sawtooth Wilderness. Many of them drag a line behind the

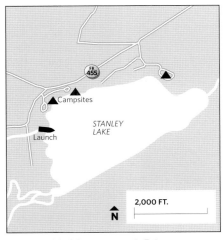

Where in Idaho? See map page 3, **F-4**

boat and troll for the stocked trout.

It can be a place to toss a small Mepps spinner or sink gear deep in search of big macs (mackinaws or lake trout), which take a lot of expertise to catch. Some of the lake trout can range from 10 to 15 pounds. It's also a fair fishery for kokanee salmon.

It's a good place for kids because they can fish for hatchery trout from the bank with a bobber and a worm or by dragging a Panther Martin behind a raft.

The scenery and camping make this a busy place in the summer. To get a campsite you better have a reservation (www.reserveamerica.com).

## UPPER PAYETTE LAKE

### Quick facts
**What's there?** Rainbow trout
**Nearest town:** McCall
**Services:** Boat launch, outhouse
**Camping:** A nicely developed Forest Service campground is at the lake.
**Special fishing rules:** None
**Getting there:** From McCall, take Warren Wagon Road on the east side of Payette Lake about 16 miles and look for the road to the campground on your left.

### Upper Payette Lake scouting report
This 400-acre reservoir appears to have all the ingredients for great

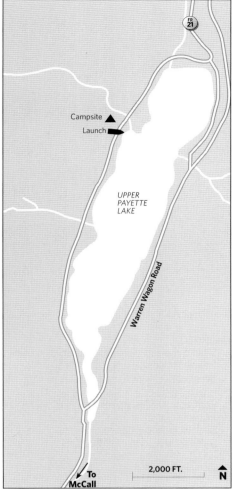

fishing, but sadly it lacks the most vital one: fish. It's stocked with rainbow trout every year, but don't expect great fishing. There's an abundance of suckers that eat whatever food might be available for trout.

But don't write it off. It's a great place to camp and it's possible to take a few trout if you work at it. There are numerous mountain lakes in the area and you can use the lake as a base camp for day trips.

You can find some trout in the North Fork of the Payette above and below the reservoir, but don't expect anything big or lots of fish. The same goes for the main Payette Lake, which is large, deep and nearly sterile. There are some huge lake trout there, which require deep trolling rigs and fish finders to catch, and occasional cutthroat and kokanee.

Upper Payette Lake is at 5,560 feet in a snow belt, so it's usually May or June before the snow clears. It's a great place to escape the summer heat because even during the hottest months, it has cool nights. Make sure to bring your bug spray because mosquitoes can be relentless, especially in spring and early summer.

Where in Idaho? See map page 3, **D-2**

## WARM LAKE

### Quick facts
**What's there?** Brook trout, hatchery trout, lake trout, kokanee salmon
**Nearest town:** Cascade
**Services:** Private rental cabins, campgrounds with outhouses, boat launch, swimming areas
**Camping:** U.S. Forest Service campgrounds
**Special fishing rules:** None
**Getting there:** Take Idaho 55 to Cascade and then Warm Lake Road 25 miles east to the lake.

### Warm Lake scouting report
This 640-acre lake surrounded by picturesque mountain scenery is perfect for fishing from a canoe or kayak. Some anglers like to skirt the lily pads and play around with the brook trout on a light fly rod or ultra-light spinning rod.

The lake is also well known by trollers targeting kokanee salmon or the large lake trout lurking around.

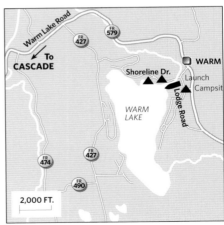

Where in Idaho? See map page 3, **D-3**

## BIG WOOD RIVER

### Quick facts

**What's there?** Rainbow trout, brown trout, whitefish

**Nearest town:** Bellevue

**Services:** Stores and gas in Bellevue, Hailey and Ketchum

**Camping:** Limited developed sites

**Special rules:** There are multiple regulations for different sections of the creek. Check the current rules booklet.

**Getting there:** Take U.S. 20 from Mountain Home and follow it to the river east of Magic Reservoir, where the river turns north and parallels Idaho 75.

## Scouting report

The Big Wood gets overshadowed by nearby Silver Creek, but it also has good trout fishing and one of the longest seasons in the state. Big Wood's trout are typically smaller than Silver Creek's, but they're not as finicky.

It's a relatively small river that's easy to wade, which is great for fly fishing. It's also fun water for fishing spinners and similar lures. If you're bait fishing, check the rules booklet because bait is not allowed in some sections of the river.

You may want to avoid it in the spring because of heavy runoff. It comes into its prime in June or July, depending on the snowmelt.

It also offers good late-season fishing thanks to its abundant midge or "snowfly" hatches that keep fish feeding throughout winter.

In the lower reaches, you're likely to find browns and rainbows, some of which move in and out of Magic Reservoir. The upper river is a classic mountain stream with a short growing season and smaller fish.

In between, the river flows through or near Bellevue, Hailey and Ketchum, which means there's lots of private property, but there is reasonably good access in many places.

The Big Wood has excellent early- and late-season fishing.

## BOISE RIVER

### Quick facts
**What's there?** Rainbow trout, brown trout, smallmouth bass, whitefish, steelhead
**Nearest town:** Boise
**Services:** Everything
**Camping:** Urban RV parks
**Special rules:** There are some size restrictions. Check the current rules booklet.
**Getting there:** The best access is between Lucky Peak Dam and Eagle. Access gets more difficult in the lower river below Star.

### Scouting report
The Boise River is an interesting piece of fishing water. It runs through the middle of Idaho's largest metropolitan area, yet sustains a good trout fishery.

Fish and Game liberally stocks it with rainbow trout and there are self-sustaining populations of wild rainbows and browns.

Catching planted trout is relatively easy. They're stocked near parks, bridges, and other places where there is easy access. These fish will take bait, lures or flies.

The wild fish are another matter. The river gets lots of fishing pressure, and wild fish are wily, elusive and difficult to catch. Every year the Boise produces trophy-sized browns and occasionally rainbows.

But the real trophy fishing takes place in the fall when Fish and Game stocks about 1,000 steelhead that are trapped in Hells Canyon. These 4- to 10-pound fish hit the river in November and are followed by a frenzy of fishing activity. During years of good salmon returns, Fish and Game may also stock chinook salmon in spring or early summer.

The river also has a healthy population of whitefish. Downstream of Star, the river habitat becomes more suitable for smallmouth bass.

The Boise River is popular because it's convenient for residents of the Treasure Valley and can have some good fishing. But it can be one of the most fickle rivers you will ever encounter. It can have good fishing one day and appear void of any fish life the next.

## MIDDLE FORK OF THE BOISE RIVER

### Quick facts
**What's there?** Rainbow trout, cutthroat trout, bull trout, whitefish
**Nearest towns:** Boise, Atlanta
**Services:** After you leave Boise, they're few and far between. There's no gas for sale in Atlanta, so plan accordingly.
**Camping:** A few small developed campgrounds and lots of undeveloped spots

near the river

**Special rules:**
There are size restrictions on the upper river above the North Fork confluence. Check the current rules booklet.

**Getting there:**
From Boise, take Idaho 21 past Lucky Peak to the Middle Fork Road, which is on the right after the high bridge.

### Scouting report

The Middle Fork is not as famous or accessible as the South Fork and doesn't produce as many, or as big, fish. But you shouldn't overlook it.

It has about 50 miles of quality trout water that is relatively accessible by a road that winds along its course all the way to its headwaters. A few words of caution: The road becomes a washboarded nightmare in the summer. It's a bumpy ride, to say

the least, and there are lots of blind corners that can be nerve-racking.

The Middle Fork has a healthy population of wild trout. It's easy to wade and the water is easy to read. Trout are commonly found in the riffles and deeper holes, which are easy to spot. This is classic spinner-fishing water and fish are also susceptible to high-floating attractor flies, especially during summer and fall.

The Middle Fork is mostly free-flowing (there's a small dam at Atlanta), but it acts like a natural river. That means it has heavy spring runoff from snowmelt in its headwaters and usually doesn't come into its prime until mid-June.

The lower river can get warm in late summer, which makes fish abandon their usual hangouts and move upstream or into tributaries to seek cooler water.

Beware of special rules for bait and barbless hooks in the upper river, and if you catch a bull trout, it must immediately be released unharmed.

## MIDDLE FORK OF THE SALMON RIVER

### Quick facts

**What's there?** Cutthroat trout

**Nearest town:** Stanley

**Services:** None. It's backcountry fishing. Bring everything you need.

**Camping:** There's a Forest Service camp ground at Boundary Creek, but it will be congested during summer because it's a launch site for floaters.

**Special fishing rules:** Catch and release only.

**Getting there:** From Stanley go west about 20 miles on Idaho 21 (or 36 miles east from Lowman) to the marked turnoff to Boundary Creek. Take Forest Roads 579 and 568 (Fir Creek and Boundary Creek), which lead to the Boundary Creek boat launch.

### Scouting report

The Middle Fork is one of Idaho's

strongholds for west-slope cutthroat trout. Fishing is restricted to catch and release, so check tackle restrictions in the current regulations.

The river is difficult to get to until the snow melts. Expect high water into June and maybe July. When it settles, it's a great place to fish.

Road access ends at the Boundary Creek boat launch. There's a trail along the river, so you can hike downstream and access numerous fishing spots. The Middle Fork is a medium-sized river, so you can wade in some areas, but be prepared for some deep water and lots of rapids.

The cutthoat are pretty gullible fish. They will readily rise to an attractor pattern or strike a spinner.

They are also migratory and tend to move farther downstream as the summer turns to fall, but you can usually find fish if you're willing to hike.

## NORTH FORK OF THE BOISE RIVER

### Quick facts

**What's there?** Rainbow trout, cutthroat trout, whitefish, protected bull trout
**Nearest towns:** Idaho City, Atlanta
**Services:** Idaho City has full services. Atlanta has limited services and no gas for sale.
**Camping:** Some developed Forest Service sites and lots of undeveloped spots
**Special rules:** None

**Getting there:**
From Idaho City travel north on Idaho 21 for 2 miles to Granite Creek/Rabbit Creek Road (Forest Service Road 327) and take it about 17 miles to the river. For the upper river, you can continue up Idaho 21 to Edna Creek and take Forest Service Roads 384 and 328 to the river.

## Scouting report

Like the Middle Fork, this is a beautiful mountain stream with plenty of trout, but it's managed differently than the Middle Fork. It has general stream seasons and rules, which means you can keep the trout you catch there (except bull trout). The river has good road access, but also roadless sections that require a hike to get to.

It's a little smaller than the Middle

Fork, so it's easy to wade and easy to read. It's a clear, cool stream that's a great place to fish during the summer.

You can expect smaller and fewer trout than the Middle Fork. Fish and Game stocks the North Fork with catchable trout, typically right before the season opens and usually before the Fourth of July, so the fish are more likely to be caught.

The North Fork is a good river for small spinners and attractor flies. Trout tend to be aggressive and will chase those lures.

Bait fishing is allowed there, and drifting a worm through a deep hole might get you some fish. If those spots are easily accessible by road, they can get fished out pretty quickly.

If you like to hike and fish, there are opportunities below where the Rabbit Creek Road reaches the North Fork, and upstream from Deer Park Campground.

## OWYHEE RIVER (OREGON)

### Quick facts
**What's there?** Brown trout, rainbow trout
**Nearest town:** Adrian, Ore.
**Services:** Fishing licenses are available at the Adrian grocery store. There's a small store/restaurant at Lake Owyhee State Park above the dam.
**Camping:** Undeveloped sites along the river
**Special rules:** Catch and release only for brown trout.
**Getting there:** Cross the Snake River on Roswell Road east of Parma to Adrian, Ore. Go north and then follow the signs toward Lake Owyhee State Park, which will take you to the river.

### Scouting report

The Owyhee River is one of the best brown trout fisheries in the Northwest and a popular spot for fly anglers from Southwest Idaho. Because it's fast becoming a regional destination, it can get crowded during prime times.

The river flows through a scenic rocky canyon and is easily accessible from a nearby road. The Owyhee is best in spring and fall, but you can catch a fish in it nearly any time of year.

The river's brown trout population is self-sustaining and because harvesting them is not allowed, they grow large. These prolific surface feeders also feast on almost year-round bug hatches. The result is plenty of fish in the 20-inch range.

The Owyhee gets year-round pressure, so the fish are smart. Anglers who can match an insect hatch and naturally present a dry fly do very well here. If fish aren't rising, nymphs and streamers catch a lot of trout. The river can be fickle. You can go hours without hooking a fish and then hook several when they go on the bite.

## SALMON RIVER

### Quick facts
**What's there?** Steelhead, chinook salmon, rainbow trout, cutthroat trout, whitefish, bull trout, smallmouth bass

**Nearest towns:** Riggins and Whitebird on the lower river. Stanley, Challis and Salmon on the upper river.

**Services:** Lots of access points along the highways.

**Camping:** Several campgrounds near Riggins and Whitebird and numerous ones on the upper River between Stanley and Salmon.

**Special rules:** They vary, so check the current rules for the section you're fishing.

**Getting there:** Take U.S. 95 north to the Riggins/Whitebird area for the lower river. Take Idaho 55 the Banks-to-Lowman Highway to Lowman, or Idaho 21 to Lowman, then continue on Idaho 21 to Stanley to the upper river.

### Scouting report
The Salmon is one of the longest undammed rivers in the United States. It flows next to roads and highways in its headwaters, then 100 miles through the Frank Church-River of No Return Wilderness and back through a roaded section near Riggins before descending through another large roadless area and joining the Snake River.

It's best known for its fall steelhead runs and spring chinook salmon runs.

Steelhead typically start arriving in September and stay in the river until the following spring. Prime fishing time starts in late September and typically lasts into December, then picks up again in February through April.

The Little Salmon near Riggins also has excellent spring steelhead fishing and so does the upper river.

Chinook salmon arrive in the spring, with May and June being the peak months for fishing depending on the timing of spring runoff.

Trout fishing is best in the upper river between Challis and Stanley, where Fish and Game frequently stocks rainbow trout. There are special regulations on which fish you can keep, so check the current rules.

There are fewer trout downstream when you get around Riggins and the lower roaded stretch, but that area offers some good smallmouth bass fishing downstream from Riggins in summer.

Jetboats, rafts and driftboats are commonly used on this river. The Salmon alternates between big, splashy rapids and long placid stretches interrupted by riffles and small rapids. Make sure you know which section you're on before you launch a boat.

There's good bank access in the upper and lower roaded sections of the river. The lower river is much broader, but bank anglers still catch a lot of fish there.

## SILVER CREEK

### Quick facts
**What's there?** Rainbow trout, brown trout

**Nearest town:** Picabo

**Services:** Gas station, store and restaurant at Picabo

**Camping:** Semi-developed spots near Idaho Fish and Game's Hayspur Hatchery and undeveloped sites upstream at Point of Rocks

**Special rules:** There are multiple regulations for different sections of the creek. Check the current rules booklet.

**Getting there:** From Mountain Home, take U.S. 20 about 80 miles to the creek. Look for signs after crossing the intersection with Idaho 75.

### Scouting report
Silver Creek draws people from all over the world to match wits with whip-smart rainbows and browns. The Nature Conservancy's Silver Creek Preserve offers anglers excellent access to prime fishing waters, where you can watch dozens of 16- to 20-inch trout cruise through the crystal-clear water.

But getting them to take your fly is another matter. Silver Creek has abundant insect hatches and the fish are totally keyed into them. Knowing the bugs and how to effectively imitate them is the key to success. Insects can be so prolific at times that it's hard to spot your fly among the real ones. There can be multiple concurrent hatches of different insects to make things even more confusing.

If you can hit the creek only one time out of the year, make it during the brown drake hatch in late May or early June. The fish go nuts for these big mayflies.

Many anglers stop at one of the many fly shops in Ketchum to hire a guide.

Silver Creek is not the best place for casual anglers, but it's not impossible to catch a fish there.

## SNAKE RIVER

### Quick facts

**What's there?** Smallmouth bass, sturgeon, catfish, carp, steelhead, trout (in Hells Canyon)

**Services:** Lots of boat ramps, Three Island Crossing State Park, Celebration Park

**Camping:** Three Island State Park at Glenns Ferry and Celebration Park south of Kuna have campgrounds. There are undeveloped camping spots along the river.

**Special rules:** Open year-round.

**Getting there:** Good access points at Walters Ferry, Marsing, Grandview, Homedale and Nyssa, Ore.

### Scouting report: Swan Falls Dam to Celebration Park

**Distance:** 9 miles
**Shuttle:** 17.4 miles
**Details:** This is arguably the most scenic float on the river.

The shuttle's fairly long, so plan for an all-day trip. There are a couple of minor rapids. Anybody with a river-worthy craft and some experience can handle them. But remember, the Snake is a broad, powerful river at all times, and flipping a canoe

could mean a long swim. The afternoon winds can be brutal, so get an early start or give yourself plenty of time. It could be done as an overnighter.

### Scouting report: Celebration Park to Walters Ferry
**Distance:** 5.5 miles
**Shuttle:** 7.7 miles
**Details:** The put-in and take-out are paved and it's an easy vehicle shuttle between the two. There are numerous large islands in this stretch, and it's less developed than much of the river downstream.

### Walters Ferry sportsman's access to Bernard Landing (off of Idaho 78)
**Distance:** 5 miles
**Shuttle:** 5.7 miles
**Details:** The north bank is less developed than the south. There are several large islands and lots of side channels and coves. This is a good stretch for watching wildlife and catching some fish. It's not a good place to cover a lot of miles because the current is slow.

### Scouting report: Walters Ferry sportsman's access to Marsing sportsman's access
**Distance:** 10 miles
**Shuttle:** 11 miles. From Walters Ferry Sportsman's Access, go right on Idaho 78

and right on South Bruneau Highway. Watch for a small brown sign on the right after the Hope House. The road takes you to the Sportsman's Access, a paved boat ramp and outhouse.

**Details:** Consider this an all-day float and watch the weather. If the wind is blowing, it can push you upstream faster than the current will carry you downstream. You may be doing a lot of rowing.

### Scouting report: Marsing sportsman's access to Marsing Island Park

Distance: 4 miles
Shuttle: 4 miles
**Details:** The boat ramp in Marsing is at Marsing Island Park, which is right below the bridge on the southwest side of the river. The park has a pond, restrooms, picnic area and paved boat ramp. Expect to be within sight of homes.

### Scouting report: Trapper Flat to Marsing

Distance: 7 miles
Shuttle: About 8 miles
**Details:** Launch at Trappers Flat on Map Rock Road on the north side of the river and go to Marsing Island Park. The shuttle will be from Trapper Flat; take Map Rock road downstream and go left on Deer Flat Road and right on Chicken Dinner Road, which will take you to Marsing Road. Go left on Marsing Road and cross the bridge. The take-out is at Marsing Island Park.

## SOUTH FORK OF THE BOISE RIVER

### Quick facts
**What's there?** Rainbow trout, bull trout, whitefish
**Nearest town:** Mountain Home
**Services:** Boat launches and outhouses on the river
**Camping:** Several semi-developed spots along the river
**Special rules:** No bait allowed, single barbless hooks and harvest restrictions.
There are also special fishing seasons. Check the current rules booklet.

**Getting there:** From Mountain Home take U.S. 20 to Anderson Ranch Dam Road and follow it downstream from the dam. To get to the upper river, continue on U.S. 20 to the Pine/Featherville Road and take it above Anderson Ranch Reservoir.

### Scouting report

The South Fork is a fly angler's dream river. It has lots of trout and whitefish and prolific and predictable insect hatches.

The most popular part of the South Fork is the dam-fed section between Anderson Ranch Dam and Danskin Bridge about 10 miles downstream. Below Danskin, the river flows into a roadless, rapid-filled canyon that is accessible only by whitewater boaters.

The South Fork has a thriving rainbow trout population and trophy-sized fish that frequently top the 20-inch mark.

The river also is open for fishing about 10 months out of the year, so the fish get a lot of pressure and are wily and skittish.

Fishing on the South Fork is largely regulated by the flows from the dam. During fall and winter, the flows are usually between 300 and 600 cfs, which make it a friendly river for wading, but too rocky and shallow for boating.

During the summer irrigation season, the flows are typically between 1,000 and 1,500 cfs, which is better for floating.

Most of the floating takes place in the 5-mile section below the dam to a take-out known as Indian Rock. Below that, the river goes through a series of rocky rapids that many boaters avoid.

The stretch below Anderson Ranch Reservoir gets the lion's share of the attention, but the upper river can be a lot of fun to fish during the summer. It's a classic swift and narrow mountain stream. While the average fish is smaller than below the dam, they're easier to catch.

---

# Southwest Idaho ponds

Merrill Pond

L ocal ponds are among the most convenient fishing spots in the area and great places to introduce youngsters and beginners to the sport. They are frequently stocked with trout and many have self-sustaining populations of bluegill, bass and other species.

At the right times, ponds can produce excellent fishing, but they also can be unpredictable. Exceptionally hot summers or frigid winters can wreak havoc on fish populations. Like most still water, spring is the best time to fish ponds. In summer, many get too warm and weed-choked. When the weed beds break down and the water cools in the fall, fishing will turn on again.

Here are 10 rural and suburban ponds to put on your short list.

Quinns Pond

## QUINNS POND (BOISE)

### Getting there

Take 27th Street between Main and State streets. Turn west on Pleasanton Avenue. There is a small parking area and access to the Greenbelt where Pleasanton dead-ends.

### Scouting report

This is more like a small lake than a pond. It has good — but not great — access for shore fishing. There are three docks that provide handicapped access and more fishing space. It's a good place to fish from a canoe, float tube or small boat.

It's located on the Greenbelt and close to the Boise River, which gives you another fishing option.

It's stocked with trout and also has bass and bluegill.

## RIVERSIDE POND (GARDEN CITY)

### Getting there

It's west of Glenwood Street just north of the Glenwood Bridge.

### Scouting report

This small pond is nestled among trees next to the Boise River, so you can fish the river, too. There's good shore access and it's close to the Greenbelt, which makes it easily accessible by bicycle. It's right off a busy street, so don't expect to get back to nature. It's frequently stocked with trout.

## MERRILL POND (EAGLE)

### Getting there

It's at Reid W. Merrill Park east of Eagle Road near Idaho 44. Take East Riverside Drive to South Shore Drive.

### Scouting report

It's a great place for kids because there's a playground next to the pond if fishing is slow. Boats and float tubes are not allowed. The Boise River is close by.

Merrill Pond is in the heart of a business district. You can fish for a while then walk to a restaurant or bar.

## SETTLERS POND (MERIDIAN)

### Getting there

It is at the corner of Ustick and Meridian roads.

### Scouting report

This small suburban pond is in a nice grassy area that provides plenty of shore access. It's another great spot to take kids because there is a huge playground and splash park. The pond is regularly stocked with trout unless it's too warm or frozen.

Settlers Pond

## SAWYERS POND (EMMETT)

**Getting there**

It is west of Emmett on Idaho 52. Turn left onto Mill Road near Milepost 30 and travel seven-tenths of a mile to Sales Yard Road. Turn right and follow Sales Yard Road for two-tenths of a mile to the pond.

**Scouting report**

It has a small boat ramp, outhouse and docks that offer good access for people with disabilities. It is a good spot to fish from shore or a small boat or float tube. It's in a rural setting if you want to get out of the city. It has stocked trout and bass and possibly some bluegill.

## DUFF LANE POND (MIDDLETON)

**Scouting report**

From Middleton, go east on Idaho 44 and south on Duff Lane to the sportsman's access sign.

**Scouting report**

It's a nice pond surrounded by shady trees. There's a dock, but bank access is limited because the banks are lined with trees and willows. It is stocked with trout and has bass and possibly bluegill. It tends to get very weedy during summer.

## WILSON SPRINGS PONDS (NAMPA)

**Getting there**

South of Nampa off South Powerline Road near the Idaho Fish and Game regional office at 3101 S. Powerline Road. From Interstate 84, take the Garrity Boulevard

Wilson Springs Ponds

exit and go south. Take a left on Flamingo Avenue and a right on Happy Valley Road. Turn right on Greenhurst Road and left on South Powerline Road.

### Scouting report

These popular ponds are great for anglers for a variety of reasons. They are generously stocked with trout. The ponds are spring fed, so they offer year-round fishing.

There's a "trophy pond" open only to catch-and-release fishing, but most ponds are open to harvest.

The area is well developed with docks, outhouses, ample parking and paths that are handicapped-accessible. Despite the development, the ponds are mostly natural and attract lots of wildlife to watch while you're fishing, especially waterfowl and songbirds.

Caldwell Pond

## CALDWELL POND

### Getting there

From Interstate 84, take Exit 26 and go west to Pond Lane. Turn left at the sportsman's access sign.

### Scouting report

It's in a rural, agricultural area and has a paved parking area with an outhouse and two handicapped-accessible docks. There are several improved bank-fishing spots. It's in a natural area with shade trees.

Trout and bass are stocked. A float tube might get you to some hard-to-reach fishing spots, but the pond is too small for boats.

## MILL POND (HORSESHOE BEND)

### Getting there
Go north on Idaho 55 through Horseshoe Bend and turn off just past Milepost 65. Look for the sportsman's access sign near the Payette River.

### Scouting report
This 11-acre pond is in a rural area, but has an outhouse, boat launch and good shore access. It's stocked with trout and is big enough for float tubes and small craft.

## WEISER POND

### Getting there
Take U.S. 95 to Weiser, turn west on Commercial Street then south on East 4th Street.

### Scouting report
This site opened in 2009 and was a community effort.

The pond is about 2 acres and ranges from 12 to 15 feet deep with a rocky shore-line and a gravel path around the perimeter. There is a wetland on the west side of the pond, and the Weiser River flows past the south side of the property.

Mill Pond

# Ice fishing

Ice fishing isn't just for grumpy old men. It's an Idaho winter tradition. Several places in the state and northern Nevada offer good ice fishing for trout and perch. Fish don't hibernate in the winter. They do get sluggish, but will feed when food is available.

Ice fishing may seem like a cold, desperate attempt to extend your fishing season, but it's more like a party on ice as anglers gather to catch a few fish, swap stories and have a picnic.

"A lot of people quit fishing in winter because it's cold out, but winter fishing can be good," said Brian Flatter, a biologist for the Idaho Department of Fish and Game.

### WHAT YOU'LL NEED

Ice fishing requires a few pieces of equipment you probably won't find in your tackle box. The first is an ice auger, which drills a 6- to 10-inch hole in the ice. Fish and Game regulations allow holes no larger than 10 inches for safety's sake.

As a rule, a smaller diameter auger bit will drill easier than a larger one, but larger holes make it easier to pull out fish.

Once a hole is drilled, you will need a slush spoon (like a jumbo version of a slotted kitchen spoon) to

keep it free of ice. A kitchen strainer may do the job a little more quickly than a slush spoon.

Since you're fishing through a small hole and won't be casting, an ice fishing rod works better than regular casting gear.

Ice rods are short, light and sensitive. A holder is a good idea to prevent an unattended rod from being pulled through the ice.

Regardless of what kind of rod you have, use the lightest line possible, but keep in mind ice is abrasive and rubbing against it can weaken line.

Another option is a tip-up rig, which is an outfit with no rod or reel that sits on the ice with a line dangling beneath it. When a fish is hooked, a flag pops up to tell you there's a fish on.

## TACTICS

The key to successful ice fishing is to roam until you locate fish. Bore a hole in the ice and spend about 15 minutes using a jig, a small piece of bait or both. If nothing bites, move on.

Ice anglers are allowed to use up to five lines, so you can try jigs and bait at different depths to locate fish. Standard trout baits — like worms, salmon eggs and PowerBait — work in the winter. Corn, mealworms, maggots, salad shrimp and cutbait also are popular. Try midwater for trout and the bottom for perch.

Part of the fun of ice fishing is you can take it as casually or as seriously as you want. On any given day, you're likely to see people decked out with portable tents, gas augers, underwater video cameras and other high-end equipment. Others will be out with a bucket and a rod.

## WHERE TO GO

Ice fishing takes place in the dead of winter, and ice on lakes and reservoirs usually is thick enough by January. The prime months are January and February.

Lake Cascade and Magic Reservoir are two of southern Idaho's most popular spots because they have trout and perch.

Wildhorse Reservoir in northern Nevada is another popular spot, but be sure to check regulations because Nevada rules are different than Idaho's.

## ICE FISHING SAFETY

➤ A minimum of 3 to 4 inches of clear, blue ice is a rule of thumb for one person on foot, but thickness is no guarantee the ice is safe.

➤ The strength of ice depends on several factors, including temperature, exposure to sunlight and underwater currents. Ice thickness and strength often vary across a lake. Four inches covering a shallow, shaded cove early in the season might support the weight of an ice-fishing party. But walking on the same spot in the spring could be courting disaster because ice weakens with age.

➤ Ice thickness from 8 to 10 inches is the minimum if you're using a snowmobile

or ATV to haul gear.

➤ If you're not sure of the thickness, drill a series of test holes on your way across the lake. Look for solid, clear ice. If in doubt, don't proceed.

➤ Avoid springs, inlets, outlets, pressure ridges or other areas where ice may be weak. Even the slightest current can inhibit freezing and create weak spots.

➤ If you're in a group, spread out across the ice when traveling and while fishing.

➤ Each person should carry a length of rope to throw in case someone falls through. Spikes that you can sink into the ice and save yourself also are a good idea.

➤ Don't carry equipment in a backpack. It concentrates weight and could encumber a person who falls through the ice. A five gallon bucket may hold all your gear and give you something to sit on while fishing. Other people prefer to load equipment onto a child's plastic sled and haul it onto the ice.

# Meet the authors

### ROGER PHILLIPS

Roger has written about the outdoors for the Idaho Statesman since 2000, and he has been camping and exploring Idaho's backcountry since 1992.

He has covered most of the state on his adventures, and he always looks forward to finding new areas of the state to explore besides returning to his old favorites.

An avid fly fisherman, Roger also enjoys many other activities, including camping, hunting, hiking, mountain biking and motorcycle riding.

### PETE ZIMOWSKY

Zimo has been exploring Idaho since he began his career as an outdoors writer and photographer 35 years ago with the Idaho Statesman.

He writes about fishing, skiing, kayaking, hiking, backpacking, hunting and camping.

Zimo jokes that he has worn out eight pairs of waders, 12 pairs of hiking boots, three kayaks, one whitewater canoe, one drift boat, and six trucks.